10-24:
A Firefighter Looks Back

Richard C. Ornberg

10-24: A Firefighter Looks Back

Published by
Eagle Mountain Promotions
1288 Summit Avenue, Ste. 107
Oconomowoc, WI 53066

ISBN-13:978-0615683508

ISBN-10: 0615683509

Cover Design by Eagle Mountain Promotions
Cover photo taken at the Illinois Firefighter Memorial, Springfield, Illinois

For Pat,
Rick, Cathy & Jason

Table of Contents

Forward

My first fire response was in 1971 hanging on a tailboard wearing a leather helmet, canvas coat, rubber boots and gloves. I rode loosely tethered to the engine by a long fabric safety belt. With one hand grasping a metal rail, I used the other to snap the front of my fire coat together while the engine bounced and weaved through traffic.

For my last fire response in 1996, I rode seated inside a fully enclosed cab. My coat, overalls, gloves and protective hood were made of space age fire resistant material and my helmet had been updated and upgraded to the point where it was now referred to as a "helmet system". I sat with my own airpack strapped to my back, seat belt buckled, and had an individual portable radio in my coat pocket.

At that first call, an injury would be treated by others on the scene with first-aid training and, if needed, an injured firefighter would be transported to the hospital in a converted panel truck outfitted with a stretcher, first aid kit and inhalator.

On my last call, that same injury would be treated in a Mobile Intensive Care Unit, manned by paramedics who could provide advanced treatment or stabilization prior to transport, all while in constant radio and telemetry contact with an emergency room physician.

I was privileged to serve 26 years on a typical large suburban fire department as it changed and evolved from the old fire service -- less than a century removed from horse-drawn pumpers -- through its transition to a modern emergency service.

As an added benefit, I began freelance writing following the old adage of "Write what you know". For me, that was the fire service. I had local experiences to work with, and as a frequent contributor to fire and emergency service publications, I drew on those of others in the region and elsewhere in the country.

This book includes many of those experiences written at the time, collected over two and a half decades, or more recently recalled and resurrected after digging through boxes during retirement.

The title "10-24" is a common emergency radio code I consider an appropriate metaphor for retired firefighters. An old first responder radio ten-code, it means "Assignment completed, ready for next response."

— Rick Ornberg, *September, 2012*

Preface

A Fire at 3:00 AM

The fire started as a small spark from the electrical outlet behind the couch. In the newly remodeled basement family room, several plugs were jammed into the small multi-plug adaptor allowing two lamps, a stereo, a clock radio, a small refrigerator and a dehumidifier to be powered from a single source. Together, the current overload collectively heated the aging and brittle plastic connector to the melting point – releasing flammable fumes that were soon ignited by the generated heat.

Within the first few minutes, the flame strained to take hold and began slowly consuming the fabric of the sofa until the dark basement corner began to glow. Once hot and burning free, the generated heat coaxed more fumes and gases from the materials nearby and the flame nourished itself further.

Increasing in size geometrically every 60 seconds, the entire basement began to fill with thick black smoke. The temperature at the ceiling started to climb toward 1,100 degrees Fahrenheit, as the heat and smoke began to stack, inching down toward the floor.

Flames now totally engulfed the sofa and embraced everything that was near. Tables, carpets, draperies, bookcases and record albums melted or ignited. Flames rolled up along a new wall and along the ceiling extending gusty jabs up the stairway leading to the rest of the house.

The top of the wooden hollow-core basement door leading to the kitchen quickly darkened and decomposed. Super heated air and smoke shot through the new opening into the kitchen while additional oxygen drawn from the upper floors provided a path to feed the growing furnace below.

The avocado green plastic kitchen phone hanging on the wall began to melt until the receiver drooped as if made of putty – until it stretched to almost a foot long. Light bulbs burst and the kitchen windows darkened with soot. Drapes began to burn and dropped onto the counter. Smoke thickened even more and moved further into the house, snaking along the ceiling, marking areas that would soon be consumed by the flames that followed. The kitchen cabinets popped into full flame in a single instant.

Awakened by a frightened dog who heard the basement windows breaking, the family of three escaped out of first floor bedroom windows and ran next door for help. The first alarm was called in and shortly, as the family watched their home slowly eaten away from the inside, they could hear the sirens approaching in the distance.

As the first fire equipment arrived, firefighters already wearing protective gear and air masks left the running boards before the engine came to a complete stop. Armed with axes and lights, two firefighters lumbered across the lawn toward the house. Others grabbed nozzles and hoses from the rear of the engine and followed, leaning into the weight of their burden. A nearby fire hydrant was quickly tapped as water pulsed through a five inch feeder to the pump on the second-in engine, which fed inch and a half hand lines leading toward the house.

"Is everybody out?" yelled one firefighter, his voice muffled by his full-face mask as he ran. After hearing the entire family was safe he joined another firefighter already at the kitchen door. At the same time, a nozzle attached to a still limp hose was played out to assure enough length was available for an initial attack. Within seconds, water forcefully pushed through the hose toward the nozzle.

Finding the front door locked, the first firefighter raised a heavy boot next to the doorknob. The combined weight of his boot and a significant dose of adrenalin obliterated the door and the jam that held it. Dropping to their knees, the firefighters moved into the doorway, straining to see or feel the direction of the fire.

Even with a powerful light the nozzleman couldn't see deeper than a few inches into the smoke, so he moved in again, now on his belly to avoid the searing heat above. By using his partially exposed ears as heat sensitive radar, he could detect a flame licking around the basement door to his left. Reaching up for the knob, he opened the door slightly as the firefighter behind him fed more hose line from behind. As the door opened, he felt a blast of heat slap him hard on the left side. Hearing the crackling sound of his own sideburn hair burning, he recoiled and grabbed an ax.

Two heavy but precise strikes of the fire ax removed the

remaining splinters of the kitchen door and the lower half of the basement door. The seat of the fire was below them, and the heat of the upper floor was still bearable enough near the floor to allow more movement inside. As the first two firefighters inched their way further into the doorway and toward the top of the stairs, others outside the house removed basement and first floor windows to allow some of the now superheated smoke to escape.

With the nozzle first set to spray a broad fog pattern, the firefighters slowly descended the stairway — it now acting more like a chimney. Sitting on each step, one at a time, they tested each step below for strength and proceeded further down. Halfway down the stairs, with the heat of the fire turning most of the water spray into steam around them, the nozzleman spotted a glow barely visible through the smoke across the basement. Narrowing the spray to a stream, he aimed a short burst at the source and moved further down. At the base of the stairs the two firefighters were connected to the safety of the outside by no more than 25 feet of inch and a half hose line. Most of the air in their tanks had been consumed, but they knew that a too-early retreat could give the fire a chance to take another hold.

On their knees and resting back on their haunches, they played the nozzle high toward the ceiling and then in a semi-circle for a few seconds for some measure of protection, then tried to pierce the darkness again with a narrowed stream of water - trying to eliminate the other random glows that would puff up throughout the still unknown floor plan.

Warning bells on both air-packs sounded almost at the same time. Only seconds of air remained – time usually reserved for making an escape. Other firefighters who had followed them in took hold of the nozzle to finish the battle, and the two exhausted firefighters made their way back up the stairs, following the hose line to the outside air.

10 minutes after the first engine's arrival, the fire was almost completely extinguished, with only small embers and hot-spots left for the crew to seek out and smother. Ceiling tiles ripped down with hooks revealed more embers, as did pried-off door jams and wall boards ripped away from their studs with axes. More lights were brought in, and the clean-up and salvage operations were underway. Care was taken to avoid disturbing too much for the eventual investigation to determine the cause and origin of the fire. The firefighters were exhausted, even though they had been working for less than an hour.

Within the first few moments of a working fire, a firefighter's pulse rate may leap from 70 to 80 beats per minute to 150 or more for a sustained period, accompanied by a severe jump in blood pressure and respirations that can consume a rated 30 minutes worth of compressed air in half that time. This rapid change can occur within 3 to 4 minutes immediately following a period of deep sleep. During the first hour of a fire, the average firefighter may exert more energy than an average laborer in a full day.

One firefighter had red, sunburn-like streaks on his neck and around his wrists. His eyes were red and puffy from smoke, heat, and the salty perspiration that had drained into his eyes. His entire uniform, contained under a heavy firefighting coat and boots, was drenched from his own sweat. Those without air packs were coughing up black phlegm and wiping black sooty mucous from their noses. Each firefighter eventually made a trip to an open engine port for a few gulps of cold water to replenish lost fluids and to help cool their insides.

As one firefighter sat slouched on the engine tailboard attempting to recover enough strength to return to work, another pulled his coat off, allowing clouds of steam to rise from his soaked clothes into the cool night air.

Now hoses had to be rolled, equipment gathered and accounted for and at least two more hours of work awaited them back at the station. Every piece of equipment had to be cleaned. air-packs refilled, fresh and dry hose repacked and vehicles readied for the next alarm. Every roll of hose used at the fire would be unrolled, washed off and hung in the stations' hose tower to dry.

One rookie firefighter wondered to himself how he could have had such a different idea of what firefighting was like. Imagined glory and adventure melted slowly to a realization that his was just a dangerous and dirty job. He silently questioned his own motives and sanity. After all, he thought, running into a building that everybody else is running out of is not a logical act.

But he felt good. Very good. No feeling he had ever experienced before compared to the feeling he had at this moment. Now with his first fire under his belt, he understood.

Chapter One

First fire

The bedclothes were folded and curled in just the right configuration for ignition. Had the cigarette fallen flat on taught and smooth bedding, chances are it would have burned away harmlessly. All that would have remained would be little more than a charred cylindrical fossil of ash where the carelessly dropped Lucky Strike had been slowly consumed.

Aided by a slight overhanging fold of material combined with the right amount of oxygen moving past the ember offering encouragement, the linen first browned, then charred until the fibers began emitting flammable fumes. An almost indistinguishable "poof" brought the small fire to its next stage.

Our two-story brick Georgian home stood in its proper rank in the midst of other similar homes unique only in brick color, painted trim and landscaping. It was 1951 and the majority of the homes in this subdivision in the northwest Chicago suburb of Des Plaines -- part of a post war housing effort that helped returning veterans and their new young families settle in with mortgages and installment plans – were still relatively new.

Interior layouts were similar too, with two bedrooms and a bathroom upstairs, a small living room, dining room and kitchen on the first floor, and a full unfinished basement. Our basement was still empty, except for a few unpacked boxes and a large pile of freshly delivered coal in the corner coal bin.

Only 4 years old at the time, I came out of my upstairs bedroom and noticed something was different as I headed toward the top of the stairway. Dark smoke was slowly rolling out of the top of my parents' partially closed bedroom door and moved along the ceiling above me.

My Father was already at work, and my Mother was most likely finishing up breakfast downstairs. No one else was in the house so I started to make my way down the stairs yelling for Mom.

"Mommy, moke! Mommy, moke," I yelled – as she would retell it mimicking my mispronunciation – while moving one step at a time down the stairs with one hand on the rail.

She raced up the stairs, passing me mid-way but quickly stopped when she saw the smoke and, feeling an instant flash of panic surge through her, realized what was happening. The smoke was already getting thicker and starting to bank lower down from the ceiling. She ran back down the stairs scooping me up on the way and plopped me down by the front door as she continued into the kitchen.

Seconds later she passed me again on her way back up the stairs carrying an aluminum pot filled with water in each hand, most of it splashing left and right with each step. Unable to reach the top since the smoke now obscured even the uppermost stairs, she decided to go back down and called the fire department for help. The number for the fire department was easier than most to remember, even several decades before 9-1-1 days. The local emergency phone number for the Fire Department was 824-1313. Rumor was that the numbers were chosen because low numbers took less time travel back and forth on the old rotary dial phones. Having made the call, she grabbed her coat and another one for me and we bolted out the front door to wait for help.

It was early January and two inches of snow covered the manicured lawns up and down the street. Each sidewalk had been shoveled the day before and only a slight residue of packed snow remained. Wrapped in an overcoat pulled over my PJ's and balancing in a pair of snow boots, I stood in the front lawn like a goose-down lawn ornament as the first firefighters passed me after jumping off the engine in front of our house. Two or three firemen, looking about 10 feet tall from my perspective, lumbered past heading for the front door with a large hose line in tow. I could hear them yelling for water then pause for an instant at the doorway. Black rolling smoke met them near the base of the stairs.

Mom and I were moved back away from the house just before we heard the sound of glass breaking above. Broken sections from the bedroom window flew out away from the house – smashing into smaller shards and pieces on the sidewalk –followed by a large column of smoke that soon was replaced by puffs of steam and jets of water as the single hose line and small smooth bore nozzle quickly extinguished the burning bed and dresser bureau.

In a matter of minutes, the excitement was over. Peering through the front door from the lawn, I could see the stairwell framed by the door. Water was rolling down each stair, soaking the thick carpeting and damming up at the front door threshold. A neighbor gathered me up at Mom's request, and I spent most of the rest of the day oblivious of the salvage and cleanup operations that were soon underway.

Within a week, carpenters had returned the bedroom to its original condition along with new coats of paint. Carpeting was replaced, and after a few days the strange and unique smell of soggy wood char finally dissipated. For a small child, it was as if nothing had ever happened.

As I grew older, I'd remember the face of the first firefighter who moved past me in the front yard, huffing from exertion as he dragged a long canvas jacketed hose. I could remember the sound of his rubber coat alternately squeaking and swishing as he moved. His wrinkled face surrounded lips that were tightly pursed -- magnifying the wrinkles and furrows of his weathered face.

That looks like a hard and dirty job, I would think as I grew up. *You'd have to be nuts to want a job like that.*

Chapter Two

Boots or Billy Club

The last thing I ever considered as a career was firefighting, and I felt that way right up to 5 minutes before taking the written exam for firefighter.

Des Plaines, Illinois in 1970 was a community of approximately 56,000 people, with an ample balance of low income, multi-family dwellings, blue collar neighborhoods and upscale housing. Along with a healthy collection of retail businesses in the downtown area and several other area shopping districts, the city was also home to a significant industrial base. Situated right on the northern border of O'Hare International Airport and at the juncture of two major interstate highways, several state routes and major railroads, Des Plaines was already a larger town than most in the state, with both visitors and employees representing a daytime population that easily bloated to over 100,000.

Although classified as a suburb, Des Plaines was actually

just another of many Cook County urban extensions of the greater Chicago metropolitan area, with only street signs and jurisdictional borders separating them. There was still one lonely farm with a cornfield remaining in town, but it was soon to be devoured by continued development, leaving only a sporadic forest preserve alongside the Des Plaines River as a small green retreat from the streets and sidewalks of a growing city.

That was the year I decided to take the exam for the Police Department, as my older brother had done several years before. Discharged from Army in 1967, I had worked various jobs, finding each of them lacking in some way. For a few years I dabbled in cartooning and drawing, hoping to get hired as a commercial artist, but without any real formal training all I could find was an extended apprenticeship with a local telephone directory publisher. It would have been good training, eventually leading to a better job, but the pay was next to nothing. As a young father of two already, waiting a year and half before drawing full salary was not an option.

At 24, I didn't think a lot about more mature concerns like extended employment benefits, retirement options or advancement opportunities. Some stability in income, however, was important. When I read that the city was holding competitive examinations for Police and Fire positions, I called to register for the exam.

My Dad was a successful corporate advertising executive, but served as a Des Plaines Police Reserve officer for several years. He died when I was 11, so even though I could still remember many of his stories he was unfortunately not there to help guide my decision. My older brother Bob, however, had been a Des Plaines cop for several years at the time, so trying out for the Police Department had been my intention when I first obtained the lengthy 12 page application form. Just days before the first written test, he felt it important to set me straight.

"Go with the Fire Department," he urged with the benefit of his years as a cop in town. "Heck, they only get a coupla fires a year, and the rest of the time they can just sit around watching TV or sleeping."

"Besides," he added, aware of my earlier loftier aspirations to become a commercial artist one day, "You can spend your downtime drawing and cartooning all you want."

That scenario sounded interesting, but I later learned that his evaluation of the fire department was still that of an outsider. Even with the promise of an abundance of downtime, the whole business of fighting fires seemed a bit scary to me. As a cop, I thought, a gun or a billy club could be a great equalizer, right?

The written exams for both the Police and Fire Department were exactly the same, word for word, with nothing uniquely job related to set them apart. Over 400 applicants showed up at the local Junior High school cafeteria to take the written examinations for either department. As I entered the cafeteria and joined the long line leading to the registration table, I glanced around and immediately felt inadequate.

Standing there in line, I recalled the feeling I had a few years earlier, in 1964, at the US Army Induction Center in Chicago. Mostly made up of draftees, that crowd was certainly larger and much more diverse, but it wasn't populated almost exclusively by those competing with each other for a limited number of openings. This room, filled with both apprehension and testosterone, had a much different feeling.

Though there were guys of all shapes and sizes, and all

of them under the age ceiling of 34, all I could see were healthy and fit-looking college-grad jocks that all looked like they came right from the gym. This was just a written exam, and only those who passed would go on to take a rigorous physical agility exam. *These guys,* I thought to myself as my place in line inched further toward the registration table, *are going to blow me away.*

The registration table was manned by one of the city's Fire and Police Commissioners, a Deputy Fire Chief and a Police Captain. Each were imposing figures; the Chief and Captain due to their crisp uniforms and command presence, and the Commissioner as an older gent in a tailored suit with a raspy, gruff voice and matching demeanor. As I came closer to the table, the commissioner was chiding a young applicant in front of me.

"Sorry son, but we have to draw the line somewhere," he grunted. The diminutive 20-something blond, practically tip-toeing to increase his height, fell back slightly in surprise.

"If I let you through because you're only a half inch short, what about the guy that comes next at only three quarters of an inch short? We gotta draw the line somewhere and sorry son, unfortunately that line is a half inch taller than you."

Not only did that send the poor guy on his way, but three others that overheard it dropped out of line as well.

As I approached the table, I handed over an already completed application that included all of my personal information, school information, references, doctor's letter, and other documents. Seeing the table tent sign "Please present current driver's license or personal identification with your application", I pulled out my license and placed it on top of the application.

"I wish you guys would take the time to complete your applications," said the Commissioner, thrusting the application back at me across the table. *Uh-oh,* I thought. *What did I forget?*

"Any idea what you're here for son?" he barked as he pointed to two empty black boxes on the front of the application, one for "POLICE" and the other for "FIRE".

"It helps if we know which department you're testing for."

Holy crap, I thought, almost instinctively making an X mark in the box next to "FIRE". *So be it. I'll go for the boots instead of a billy club.*

The commissioners kept actual names separate from the completed exams to prevent any accusations of patronage or favoritism. Since the written exam was the primary filtering device in the process, each of us filled out a form with our name, address and phone number and were instructed to place it in an envelope and seal it. On the outside of the envelope was a number. We were told only to write that number on the top of the exam form as the sealed envelopes were gathered by test monitors. Once the exams were graded, those with passing grades would be handed off to another person who would open the corresponding numbered envelopes and notify the applicant.

I was the second person in the room to complete the exam, following about 5 minutes after the first applicant brought his completed test form up to the registration table as instructed. Before I got up I checked twice to make sure I hadn't missed a page or two. The test was not that difficult – mainly a general knowledge exam to determine reading skills, tool aptitudes, comprehension skills and other basics essential to being able to absorb and retain the training that would follow. Out of the 400 or so taking the exam, with that number whittled away through subsequent testing and qualification steps, an eventual eligibility list of 20 or so would be established, ranked in order of total points. This list would be valid for three years. The Fire Department initially needed only 3 applicants from this list. Yeah right, I figured. I guess I'll keep checking the want ads.

Within two weeks, I received an official letter from the commission that I had passed the written exam, with various dates for the subsequent physical agility test, medical exam and oral interview. The agility test was the first challenge after the written exam, and we had to report on the following Saturday to Station One.

In 1970, the fire department headquarters was still just one component of an old red brick conglomerate of three attached buildings in downtown Des Plaines. The fire department – once housing horse-drawn equipment -- was on the east end, with the Police department on the west end and City Hall nestled in between. Driving past the building before parking in the alley behind, I saw the ladder truck parked out front with it's 100 foot ladder fully extended over the street. It was to be part of the agility exam.

The exam was basic. Initially designed to test for strength and agility, the test involved a minimum performance in a variety of areas. These included push-ups and pull-ups, a standing broad jump, the ability to touch your toes keeping your legs straight, a minimum number of standing weight lifts – additional presses earning extra points – and a 100 foot climb to the top of the extended ladder. The ladder climb, it could be argued, was perhaps the only test that could be defined as strictly job related, but it was in fact a test to determine if an applicant had a fear of heights.

Ladder Truck 81 at the time was an old open cab truck intended for use in warmer and dryer climates. It was the city's only ladder truck at the time, and we were told that the cab was open so that the driver cold better visualize the surroundings and buildings as he positioned the truck for operations. It was open to all weather conditions as well, so the driver, company officer and firefighters would ride outside, exposed to the elements. It was even supplied with windshield wipers on the inside of the windshield, and responding crews also brought an extra windshield scraper to remove ice and snow from both sides in the winter. The ladder's rotating base was located just behind the cab, and even when the ladder was fully retracted, it would extend out behind the truck's rear end. Extended to it's full length, the four section aluminum structure visibly swayed back and forth in the wind. From the ground we could see the topmost section, about 18 inches wide, slowly moving left and right like a stationary drunk having difficulty keeping his balance.

One or two applicants each year turned around and walked away when they saw the ladder. And each year fire officials and potential recruits wondered just what these applicants thought the job of firefighter entailed. A few others like myself, did our best to hide our apprehension. I had learned in the Army that sometimes the fear of appearing to be afraid can become powerful enough to override any actual potential risk. Few want to be the first to run away, the first to hesitate or the first to quit. At least that's what helped me climb to the top of the ladder, ring the bell as required, and climb back down.

One applicant, at 34 years old, was the oldest among us having just slipped in under the age limit of 35. He came prepared for anything. Expecting a more grueling series of tests, he wore a t-shirt and short gym shorts, so as to not limit his flexibility or overheat. The ladder truck was parked in front of the station, on the ramp which emptied onto a downtown main street, also part of a state route and always full of traffic. The ladder extended high over the ramp and street clearly becoming the highest point in the downtown area and attracting a lot of attention and gapers from passing cars. The recruit was halfway up the ladder, approaching the 70 foot level when the Captain in charge looked up to see why the passengers in a few passing cars were pointing up.

High overhead and in full view in the bright Saturday morning sunlight, it become obvious that the applicant had forgone the wearing of either underwear or jockstrap for his climb into the sky.

"Dammit," yelled the Captain. "Get up and down that ladder quick 'cause your balls are hangin' out and stopping traffic!" Adjusting his climbing technique to keep matters closer and less exposed, the candidate completed his climb.

"Never seen a guy climb a ladder side-saddle before," said the Captain as he marked the appropriate box next to the applicant's name.

In years to come, the physical agility test would be refined and honed several times to better reflect actual job related requirements, and as some suggested, to level the playing field a bit for female applicants. This created a lot of debate and accusations back and forth between traditionalists and progressives for several years. To establish a fair baseline, and to better reflect actual job requirments the department tested all personnel in several various job related activities such as dragging and lifting filled hoselines, scaling a 6 foot wall from a stationery position, carrying wieghted dummies up and down several flights of stairs, chopping actions and other activities. Each firefighter was rated, and from those ratings a baseline was established that new applicants would have to meet, male or female.

Within a few weeks, after a physical examination and a general interview by Fire and Police Commissioners, the testing process was complete. Any military service points were added where applicable and a final, ranked eligibility list was posted. Knowing there were three immediate openings, I quickly scanned the list, finding my name in the number four position. The first three were given a date to report for initial training. The rest of us would have to wait our turn until someone left the department, either through disability, retirement or death.

The Friday before the first three rookies were to report, I wondered how it would be for them on Monday and what they would experience. I was a little irritated that each of them would already be experienced firefighters or perhaps even seasoned veterans by the time my name came up. Later that same day, however, I received a phone call from the Fire Chief.

"Any chance you can start on Monday?" the Chief inquired.

The department had just terminated a probationary firefighter that day, one who that had not yet completed his first year -- a year within which a firefighter can be let go without the need of civil service hearings. Now there was a fourth opening, and the Chief was hoping I could start training with the others. I felt an obligation to at least give my present employer a week's notice, so my first interaction with the Department was to start off one week behind in training.

Though he sounded a bit disappointed, I hoped the Chief was at least impressed by my concern for my employer. That's what I wanted to believe, whether he thought so or not. I'd just have to make do with three weeks of training instead of four.

Chapter Three

What Fire Academy?

As a small department, we didn't have a formal fire academy with trained instructors, specialized classrooms and audio visual equipment, or exotic training towers. Maybe such luxuries were available in major cities like Chicago, but our training was a four week process that preceded an assignment to a duty shift. On duty officers and others were assigned to conduct training sessions in their area of expertise, or as assigned by the Fire Chief. Most of these were intense and informative, and the result of personal experience or proficiency on the part of the instructor.

In 1971, the department was just beginning a transition from the old to the new, and a formal paramedic program was still a few years away. Emergency medical calls were a secondary training priority – even if they had already started to represent the majority of actual calls.

A detailed training schedule was provided, which included fire ground operations and evolutions. Having nothing to do with Darwin, "evolutions" within the fire service involved training procedures and drills related to firefighting, tools, equipment and S.O.P.'s (Standard Operating Procedures). These included ladder operations, ventilation tools and procedures, and self contained breathing apparatus (SCBA's) training along with search and rescue techniques.

To help prepare us for duty on one of the ambulances housed in each of our three fire stations, each morning of our second week was reserved for Advanced First Aid training. This covered the basics such as Cardiopulmonary Resuscitation (CPR), fracture immobilization, bandaging, and basic diagnostic skills. Just a few years prior to this, a medical emergency response was an engine crew with a first aid kit and oxygen tank, with a local funeral home also responding in a converted hearse outfitted as a basic ambulance for transport to the hospital.

As recruit firefighters – the term "firemen" had only just recently been declared politically incorrect – we learned about ropes and knots, essential for fireground and rescue operations, and practiced in smoke filled training rooms searching for heavy dummies that we rescued and brought out into the clean air.

Intended to prepare us for the sights we'd encounter on the ambulance, a special tour was arranged for our group to spend a day at the Cook County Morgue in downtown Chicago. There, we'd observe an autopsy, and – escorted by a particularly ghoulish county worker hoping to make an impression on us – visit various storage lockers containing both recent and unclaimed corpses. He delighted in describing the reason for each body's condition, but thankfully kept silent when we passed through the "infant room", where newborns, infants and other small children lay in various degrees of decomposition. He puffed on an extremely offensive smelling cigar, explaining that it was the best way to counter the smell in certain rooms. The rest of us would need to rely on a small dollop of Vicks Vapo Rub under our nostrils. Before the day was out, he shared a particularly grizzly slide show of photos he'd meticulously gathered over the past several years, including shots of just about every grotesque arrival at the morgue's loading dock – complete with overly-descriptive narrative. Nobody passed out, and nobody threw up, so apparently our group was not as accommodating to the tour guides as some others had been.

Throughout those four weeks, we drilled, practiced and learned how to use equipment that in some cases would either be obsolete or improved on dramatically over the next few years. The breathing tanks, for example, dubbed "Air Packs", were rated for 60 or 30 minutes of air. In reality, they offered half that during a working fire. Though excellent protection against superheated air or toxic fumes, only one or two were usually available, and these were stored in large black suitcase-like boxes in one of the engine equipment compartments or in the trunk of the Chief's car. With 15 to 20 firefighters initially responding to a confirmed house fire, many would find themselves making entry and searching without the benefit of an SCBA (Self Contained Breathing Apparatus). Some oldtimers even considered the air-packs as only for specialized needs, extended interior searches or other operations. Taking the time to don an airpack, some believed, or not entering a building without one, was only for wimps. Fortunately, that antiquated attitude soon went the way of rubber gloves and canvas coats.

A four story training tower had recently been built at our western-most Station #3 and became the central location for almost all of our exterior training. It was complete with an enclosed "smoke room" for airpack training and a clear plastic tube representing a sewer manhole for rescue evolutions. We rappelled with ropes down the side of this tower, ran up and down the four flights of stairs carrying hosepacks, or carried simulated victims constructed from old hoses weighing 150 pounts or so up and down.

The tower was useful for most of our ladder training, and we took turns rescuing each other out of a third story window, or practiced hooking a ladder rung to a windowsill to anchor it so it could support a large hoseline feeding smaller attack lines inside.

One day we worked with one instructor who was either totally unmotivated, or was just having a bad day. The four of us recruits spent most of one afternoon listening to the monotone voice of a lieutenant reading aloud from a training manual. Once when he left the room to take a phone call, one of us reached over and advanced his bookmark by 3 or 4 pages. When he returned, he picked up the manual and began reading again without any pause. One could argue that, for the first time, we'd actually acted as a cohesive group, and reduced our agony by at least an hour.

In our third week, the four of us were loaded into a van and driven to the Great Lakes Naval Air Station just a few miles north. There, the Navy maintained a firefighting training course that offered us some experience battling flammable liquid fires. The term "Fog on deck" became the watchword all day as we trained alongside Navy recruits advancing hoselines in coordinated attacks and huddled with them inside a small and sooty smoke room as training officers filled the room with black smoke from burning fuel oil. We were able to leave and return to our cozy homes that night, but I almost felt sorry for the exhausted young recruits – mostly in their late teens – as they trudged back to the barracks.

We learned about engine pumps, hoselines, nozzle pressures, and even fluid dynamics in the form of "friction loss", the factor that reduced a line's pressure between the pump and the nozzle. Hoses were packed on an engine in a zig-zag pattern with the last few lengths folded and placed in such a fashion that a firefighter could grab one section and drop a several lengths of inch and a half diameter hoses as attack handlines at a fire scene. These had to be repacked the same way, of course, for the next potential fire.

All manner of hand tools were available for use at a fire scene or rescue operation, mostly carried on either an engine or a truck, and these accounted for almost two days of training or familiarization. The main difference between calling a firefighting vehicle an "engine" or a "truck" is that an engine includes a water pumping system used to boost the pressure and volume of water from a hydrant. That's when I learned that any tool or procedure could be eligible for the term "fireman proof" if it had been designed for maximum simplicity and ease of use.

After four weeks, we certainly weren't trained and competent firefighters, at least not to the degree that would be required of firefighters years later. Fire Training Academies were soon established, and at least in our state, an official training standard leading to Firefighter Certification standings would become a common prerequisite. But, armed with all the basics, some understanding of terminology and at least the ability to recognize most of the special equipment, we were assigned to a fire company. There was a lot of on-the-job training still to come, and for all of us, training was to continue regularly and extensively for the next 26 years.

At the time we were assigned to one of three shifts, designated as Red, Black or Gold. Other departments called them First, Second and Third or by other labels. Like most other departments, firefighters worked 24 hours on, with 48 hours off. Add a few additional days off during the year and that would collectively allow for, on average, a 56 hour work week.

In many parts of the country, fire departments were still were managed by the "old school" leaders who originally started as volunteers. Many of the Fire Chiefs and top administrators in the late 60's and early 70's may have been the last of those who continued on as full timers when their departments switched to full time. As volunteers or paid on call firefighters, many firefighters were bankers, lawyers, doctors and other professionals, or business owners in the community. When a department changed to become full time, those volunteers who earned the higher professional salaries or benefits typically weren't able to stay on. This meant that the initial administrative leadership in many areas fell to average blue collar workers and military veterans. My group was among the last to count several veterans as part of their number as well.

The advent of the college-educated firefighter was just around the corner.

Chapter Four

Planet Firehouse

Most outsiders would find a firehouse a completely different world, where many accepted rules of society don't seem to apply. It even takes new recruits some time to learn where they fit in, how they fit in, or even IF they fit in.

A fire recruit's treatment in a firehouse could never be considered either nurturing or considerate of his self esteem. One of the first things I learned when I came on shift was my exact position relative to a substance that I'll politely refer to as "whale dung". As a new recruit I soon learned that I inhabited a much, much lower level, and I should get used to it, and get ready to quietly accept every lowly job or chore thrown at me for much of my first year.

Every firehouse is different, but in many ways is much the same. They range in size depending on the number of engine or truck companies they house and some may also have offices or other facilities to help support training, fire prevention or administrative needs. Each has a few basic components, though, essential for efficient 24/7 fire response.

The apparatus floor houses in-service and standby fire engines, ladder trucks, ambulances and any specialized rescue or suppression equipment. Each station also has a kitchen and living area providing a place for those on duty to prepare and eat meals that are paid for at the firefighter's own expense. Those working a 24 hour shift also need a place to sleep overnight between calls, so a separate bunkroom along with toilet and showers is a must.

The dynamic among firefighters living and working together in a firehouse ranges somewhere between the heroic-men-of-action stereotypes depicted in any old Howard Hawks war film, and a group rendition of "Who's Afraid of Virginia Wolff." The firehouse becomes a second home, and those who share it become members of a family dealing with schizophrenic-like swings between mutual support, all-out war, and everything in between.

I soon learned that at any emergency scene, everyone became thier brother's keeper. It was the firefighter next to you, above you, below you, behind you or in front of you who would be the one to help you avoid serious injury or death. If you unfortunately did find yourself in a bad situation, it would be your fellow firefighters who helped get you out of it. Or, as is tragically the case sometimes, it would be fellow firefighters who would be listed with you among those injured or killed at a fire.

Much of the time, however, a firehouse is an isolated and unique environment steeped in history and local tradition, tempered by schedules and routine. Sometimes, during a long stretch between fires, some tensions could grow and result in a squabble or two, but one good fire would quickly erase them. Nobody has ever come up with a better way of releasing tension than smashing and breaking things – with a purpose and as necessary, of course.

Living as a unit in a firehouse on shift placed each of us into a new family. Firefighters found themselves spending more time with those on their shift than they did with their own families at home. Firehouse speech patterns, where profanity reached a level I'd never even experienced even while in the Army, were often hard to control when outside the firehouse. Within the confines of any firehouse, The "F" word often replaced any and all punctuation in conversation, sometimes even used in the middle of words, such as "in-f***ing-credible", or "out-f***ing-standing!"

The most common work schedule for career firefighters is a 24 hour on, 48 hour off, arrangement. Since that can translate into either a 48 or a 72 hour work week, a designated number of off days are scheduled each year -- some departments call them "Kelly Days" -- in an attempt to bring the hours to 54 or 56 hours per week on average. Firefighters working this schedule are assigned to one of three shifts.

The 24 on, 48 off schedule traditionally works so well because the on-duty firefighters can stay at the station overnight, still on duty and fully prepared for an emergency response. If they were scheduled on 8 hour shifts similar to the Police Department and other 24 hour service providers, then the Fire Department would have to fully man four shifts instead of three. As with any round-the-clock service, someone always needs to be off duty, or on vacation or holiday. The bunks in the firehouse essentially remove the need for a fourth shift and save a ton of taxpayer dollars in personnel costs each year.

A typical firehouse usually included a fully equipped kitchen, bathrooms and showers, sleeping quarters, and a dayroom for downtime. Divided over three shifts, a group of 8 to 14 men worked together and lived together and also shared facilities with two other shifts that preceded them or followed them. It was not uncommon to walk into a firehouse kitchen and see three separate refrigerators and food cabinets located side by side, each locked with a padlock.

As it still does today, everything in a firehouse revolves around response to emergency calls, or staying prepared to do so. Monday through Friday may have designated work schedules, essential for apparatus and building maintenance, on-going training and perhaps even some fire and safety inspection duties performed as a company within the district. Saturdays might be set aside for more intensive apparatus maintenance and testing of equipment. Evenings, Sundays and holidays, with the exception of emergency calls, were usually a "stand-by" schedule, open for firefighters to rest, watch TV, study, or sleep if they're lucky. For many departments fifty percent or more of the calls they log within a year are between the hours of 8 pm and 8 am the next morning, so a night's sleep is not always a sure thing.

Since firefighters eat in the station and prepare their own meals, everyone kicks in a few bucks in the morning to cover the cost of meals. One firefighter might be sent to a grocery store to shop, or an engine or ambulance crew might be sent to a store within the district to shop with portable radio in hand, ready to respond. Many times a crew may be forced to leave a fully loaded shopping cart mid-way through checkout and run out of the store to respond to an emergency. Most stores are very understanding and will set the groceries aside for their return later.

Most develop the habit of eating fast, since many times a crew will sit down to a well cooked meal -- thanks to the skill of the firefighter-cook that day -- only to be interrupted by an emergency call. By the time everyone returns to the station, food can be cold or even ruined. So once it's on the plate, knives and forks flash back and forth, dishes may be passed laterally and across the table quickly, and a simple request to "pass the @&#% salt" can result in a flying salt shaker passing like a missile from one end of the table to the other.

Bunkrooms vary in size and degree of privacy, if any. Ours resembled a typical Army barracks set up of bunks lined up on either side of an aisle. Today, many bunkrooms have dividing walls, bed tables and lamps, and power outlets. Some would try to hit the sack early in the evening to "bank" a few hours in expectation of one or more overnight calls. Others would wait until later, and a few even avoided the bunkroom altogether, spending the night on a dayroom couch or recliner. After a year or so of waking up with several paper-wrapped rolls of toilet paper around my bunk -- thrown at me throughout the night by those trying to stop my snoring -- I became a day-roomer myself, both as a courtesy to others and in self-defense.

One rite of passage for many recruits on shift is the eventual assignment of a nickname. Nicknames might evolve or be assigned, always adopted or established in good fun. It's not an official act but seems to just happen over time. Some are earned right away; others may take even a year or so to develop. For those who are so tagged, the nickname can be either one to be proud of or one that causes embarrassment. Either way, it sticks, and can follow a firefighter for their entire career.

The shifts became populated with names such as Blinky, Shingles, HoHo, Reptile, and Swanee, One nickname of Rocks, was adapted for a younger recruit who reminded us of Rocks, so he was named Pebbles. Others included Canary, Gus, Rollie, CJ7, The Duck, Flippy, Pro, Booby, Kagoots, Killer, Trip and Smokestack. One large framed firefighter was nicknamed Mongo for his size. He was also known as Bing, or sometimes by the more formal version "Bingus-Galacticus". Most had a distinct story behind them, but some were just variations or different spelling of an existing name.

One time a couple of self-appointed nicknames backfired. In the early days of the paramedic program, two partners on Ambulance 71 playfully adopted the names of "Gage" and "Desoto", the two main characters - both paramedics -- on a popular TV show at the time called "Emergency". As a gag, they even went so far as to buy black plastic nametags with those names and they wore them from time to time on shift.

A year prior, both of them had responded to a violent domestic disturbance that resulted in the eventual death of the victim. As the attending and transporting medics on that call, it wasn't a surprise when a year later they would be called in for an interview by law enforcement as a trial had been scheduled. In this case, however, there was some question regarding possible excessive use of force by the police, and investigators requested an interview with them. Since the firefighters involved were on shift, they drove to the Police station with the ambulance to be interviewed.

For the cops this was serious business, and it was important that both paramedics stick to the truth as they recalled it, and behave professionally. Once inside the interview room, one of the detectives began filling out an interview form, having entered in the date, time and location. He took their names and then, looking up and down a couple of times, noted that the names they gave and the names on their nametags didn't match. It took a while to explain all of this to the detectives. After having to make a few telephone calls, the detectives, not blessed with the firefighters' sense of humor, proceeded with the interview. The names Gage and Desoto didn't show up on anyone's shirt after that.

Firefighters in a firehouse can gossip more than anyone. We picked on each other at the table and picked on those at other stations. We picked on the off duty shifts and we picked on those in other departments. We picked on the Police Department and on our own officers and Chiefs. We picked on anything that moved. Big city departments picked on small town departments, career firefighters picked on volunteers, and vice versa. But, because of the bond that exists among all firefighters, nobody from the outside was allowed to pick on anyone. Ever. Period.

The firefighter's bond with other firefighters is a powerful and universal dynamic. While tensions can build over time in the relative close proximity of a firehouse environment, nothing becomes more intimate than the shared experience of firefighting or a hazardous rescue operation. Big city or small town, career of volunteer, two firefighters crawling together completely blind in a superheated and toxic atmosphere, connected to the outside world only by a length of inch and a half hose line learn a lot about each other, and depend on each other for their lives. Firefighters share experiences that reveal their hidden strengths and expose individual weaknesses. Working together this way creates an intimate bond that quietly but firmly underlies the connection between firefighters worldwide.

Chapter Five

The Superman Suit

Firefighting gear in the early 70's adhered more to tradition than reality. It continues to evolve today as it has over a couple of centuries. When I started on the department in 1971, we were issued black canvas coats, a standard leather fire helmet, boots that pulled up over the thighs, a truckman's belt, and rubber gloves. These basic components offered limited protection against a variety of potential injuries but were far from what firefighters wear today.

The canvas coats, similar to those worn by sailors in rough seas decades before, had metal clips up and down the front to close the coat and a thick collar that would pull up to offer some protection to the neck. The leather helmet offered limited impact protection from falling debris, but had no chin strap to secure it, no built in eye protection, and served mainly to allow water to flow freely off the helmet and off the extended lip on the back. Most of us were also issued plastic flip-down eye protectors that we installed under the front visor of the helmet. We would flip these down to keep debris out of our eyes during overhaul operations such as opening up walls or pulling down ceiling tiles to check for flames or embers.

Our fireboots were equipped with steel toe guards, steel shin protectors and steel mesh protection in the soles to protect against nails or other sharp objects. The gear included a handy truckman's belt, which served many purposes. In addition to carrying gear at your side, you could wrap one end of the belt around a large handline hose and slip the other end over your shoulder for greater control.

All this protective gear was topped off with a pair of bright orange rubber gloves. Woolen inserts were also provided for the cold winters in Des Plaines.

As the fire service reporting policies and procedures evolved nationally, a growing number of injuries were statistically attributed to failures of some protective gear. As statistics often do, they stimulated more interest on the part of municipalities that covered the medical costs for potentially avoidable injuries. Gear suppliers, of course, caught on and were quick to develop and market even more improved gear when cities and towns started upgrading.

Canvas coats and rubber gloves were soon replaced by space-age Nomex or other fire resistive fabrics. Hip boots were soon replaced by shorter boots that would be worn with new fire resistive overalls and new coats. Helmet design and innovations soon followed offering greater impact resistance, built-in vision shields -- designed to be able to pull down over a self contained breathing apparatus mask -- and fire resistant ear flaps offering greater protection on both sides of the head and the back of the head. Many departments added a new item, initially the source of some controversy for some veteran firefighters, in the form of a full nomex hood pulled over the firefighter's head. This was adapted directly from NASCAR type racing gear. Veteran firefighters didn't like them at first because they no longer could use their ears to detect radiant heat from a fire and pinpoint its source. (Described in greater detail further on.)

For an actual fire attack, however, no single item is as important as the airpack, providing a rated 30 or 60 minutes of air in a deadly and toxic environment. In addition to superheating the air in a burning room, the thick and acrid smoke contains just about every poisonous substance you can think of, including cyanide and other chemicals depending on what's burning. One whiff of most of these gases will immediately incapacitate and kill anyone unprotected.

Again, Hollywood has painted a false picture of firefighting when it depicts the hero taking a deep breath before entering a room on fire and weaving through areas of flame to reach the damsel in distress. In a real fire, he wouldn't be able to see his hand in front of his face, much less even open his eyes. Even when the hero grabbed a towel or rag to hold in front of his face, the first whiff would stop him immediately. Most smoke in a fire doesn't just choke you, it burns and stings the exposed mucus membranes inside your mouth, nose, and eyes. Imagine trying to inhale or swallow a super hot chunk of steel wool the size of a tennis ball, and it's easy to understand the term "....but was driven back by the thick smoke." It's as much of a barrier as a brick wall.

A lot of firefighter training revolves around or includes the air pack. Since the device involves a large metal tank strapped on a firefighter's back, there are even times when it may need to be removed in a smoke-filled room. One training scenario involves a firefighter with airpack passing from one area to another -- a possible escape evolution -- through a relatively small opening or hole that would not be large enough to allow the firefighter wearing a tank on his back to pass through. This exercise requires the firefighter to remove the air tank from his back, while still wearing the facemask providing clean air of course, and while still attached to it by a short breathing hose. He has to pass the tank through the hole first and crawl through after, re-donning the airpack once on the other side.

In a smoke filled training room, it's hairy enough to accomplish, but in the frenzy of an actual fire it would be a last-resort choice for anyone. I remember commenting that if faced with the real situation, "...they'll probably find me dead, after trying to find a larger hole."

For me the firefighting gear was my Superman suit. I knew that it offered some protection against some injuries, but it became more of a psychological security blanket in many ways. Wearing the gear usually coincided with the typical adrenalin rush that accompanies many emergency responses, so my endurance, strength and stamina were usually greater when in the gear than otherwise. Donning the gear almost became a Pavlovian stimulant, emergency or not.

Just before entering a burning building, we'd usually crouch down by the chosen entry point in our full firefighting gear. With thick black smoke belching out of the opening we would pull the air mask over our heads, don the helmet, strap it under our chin, and move in on hands and knees to seek out either the seat of the fire or search for occupants. Once we were past the early years where airpacks were "just for wimps" it was simple. No Superman suit, no entry.

A fully equipped firefighter, dressed for entry into a fire, is a striking image. Coupled with the Darth Vader breathing sounds, the image can be downright startling. So much so that a few of us actually appeared on Chicago's Bozo the Clown Show in a segment showing kids the gear and how a firefighter looked and sounded at a fire. The hope was that the kids would see us as helpful friends and not scary monsters and not hide from us as we searched their home.

There was one time, however, when one woman acted as if all the gear was totally invisible.

Working out of our south side Station #2, we responded with an engine to a trouble alarm at a restaurant about 7 blocks down the street. SOP (Standard Operating Procedure) was that responders wear full firefighting gear until investigating the cause of the alarm. We drove the 7 blocks, lights and siren, donning our coats, air tanks and helmets along the way.

After pulling up in front of the restaurant, and seeing no sign of smoke or problems, the engine officer and I went in the front door to investigate -- each of us in full gear, with air tanks on our backs and helmets on our heads. Inside the door and about 20 feet down the entry way, we approached the hostess podium, manned by a middle aged woman who, seeing us approach, grabbed two menus and asked, "Will that be two for lunch?"

The new gear also brought new challenges to some of us firefighters used to fighting fires in the older gear. Sure, the updated apparel provided greater protection but it created some problems as well.

For starters, the full encapsulation in the heavily insulated fire resistive fabrics could take a toll on first responders by retaining heat as well has resisting it. In warmer weather some firefighters would find they were drenched in their own sweat by the time they stepped off a responding engine. Entering heated environments and crawling along the floor where the ceiling temperature a few feet above is approaching 1100 degrees Fahrenheit could dehydrate a firefighter in minutes, affecting performance as well as judgment.

The newer mandate of the NASCAR variety Nomex hoods, pulled over the head before donning a fire helmet, certainly offered greater protection to the ears and neck areas formerly exposed to heat, flame and steam. For some veterans the extra coverage also blocked some of the sensory input firefighters depended on in a fire scene where thick smoke renders them totally blind. Up until then firefighters entering a structural fire on their hands and knees used their exposed ears as a way to help determine the location of the fire in a smoke filled room. By turning the head to the left or the right, the amount of heat felt on the exposed ears was a "radar" of sorts, at least helping to determine the direction of the greatest heat. It was a simple dynamic: Turn your head to the left and only your right ear is hot, and then turn to the right until your left ear feels heat, and you've at least pinpointed the direction of the hottest area. The protective hoods offered greater protection but also masked or diminished some senses used for blind navigation.

Another unanticipated result was that while the combined improvements in more protective apparel and breathing apparatus increased effective use from 20 minutes to 40 minutes and increased the amount of time a firefighter could remain inside during an interior attack, there was an increased exposure to hazards as well. Instead of the initial attack into a fire being limited by an air tank alarm bell signaling diminished air, firefighters were able to forge further and deeper into a burning structure. That helped increase the area that could be covered in a primary search, but also lengthened the time needed for any escape or route of retreat should things get out of hand.

With the improved gear, we could spend more time in a toxic or heated environment. Rubber gloves, up until then sufficient for most needs, didn't stand up too well when working in a fire for longer periods of time. Exposed to too much heat, the rubber gloves could melt, causing even more serious burn injuries to the wearer. At one point, even as our other turnout gear improved, we found ourselves still using the older orange rubber gloves. Once we presented samples of burned melted rubber gloves worn by one of our own firefighters to our city council's safety committee, new Nomex protective gloves were quickly ordered for each firefighter.

As evident in firefighter injury statistics since the 1980's, there's no doubt that the improvements in gear and equipment have saved lives and prevented injuries in addition to increasing fire suppression efficiencies. Over time, training and experience continues to help firefighters balance those new protections with updated and adapted suppression and rescue techniques.

Chapter Six

Pit Bulls

"Structure fire, second floor apartment, 310 N. Seegers Road. Smoke showing, caller says people trapped on second floor."

Nothing gets the adrenalin pumping quicker than a report of smoke or flames showing, but with someone possibly trapped on an upper floor the dose is even higher. When that alarm came in, I was riding backwards on Engine 61, which I knew was most likely going to be the first engine in, with our ladder truck close behind. At least the ground ladders on our engine should be sufficient for any initial exterior rescue, if needed. The call was in an area known locally as Hawaiian Village, simply because of street names such as Luau Drive, Waikiki Drive, Polynesian Drive and so forth -- clearly out of place in an area of several low income apartment buildings populated mostly by immigrants, transients, and minority groups. Each apartment building contained 4 apartments, two up and two down, with both a rear and front entrance off of two stairwells.

As we pulled up Lt. Jack Henley confirmed smoke

showing, and several tenants ran toward the engine as it came to a stop at the curb. We positioned ourselves closest to the building, allowing the second engine in to tap a hydrant and feed our lines if necessary. Several residents were yelling in thick Spanish and broken English that a woman and her daughter were trapped upstairs. As they did, we saw a matronly Hispanic woman and another younger woman hanging out of a second story window facing the street. They were yelling as well, but were having difficulty since they were almost engulfed by the thick black smoke that filled the window opening over them. The smoke puffed out along the back of their heads even as they stretched the upper part of their bodies out further trying to catch some clean air.

We were a three-man engine company that morning, so since Lt. Henley and I had already donned our air packs while enroute, we grabbed a 24-foot ground ladder off the engine and quickly headed for the building. After setting the ladder, and with the second engine already making entry with a line from the back entrance to the stairwell, Jack heeled the ladder while I scrambled up to the window. As I reached the window's bottom edge, the older woman was already climbing out of the window trying to gain footing on the rungs. When I reached her, I guided her feet to the rungs and breathed a sigh of relief that I didn't have to get her out of the window myself, as she clearly outweighed me. Her daughter, perhaps in her late teens or early twenties, looked like she was about to get on the ladder as well but stayed put at my urging, though she held tightly to the ladder beam as if afraid someone was about to take it away. I closed in around the mom, with my legs just below her and my arms on either side to guide her down the ladder. At first I kept close, but soon realized that I was face to face with an ever increasing pattern of urine spreading wider and wider across her backside as she moved.

Once she was on the ground, I immediately climbed back up to do the same with the girl, who literally met me halfway. As I reached her, I heard her mom just below screaming, "My babies! My babies! My babies up there!" Another adrenalin jolt kicked in. I quickly asked the daughter as I hung off to the side so she could climb down past me, "Is that right? Are there babies up there?" She nodded frantically and yelled out something in mixed English and Spanish. All I could make out was "in the bathroom!" Once she cleared me on the ladder, I hooked a leg around a beam and pulled on my air mask, tightened the straps, and was over the top of the ladder into the window in seconds, hitting the floor inside on my hands and knees.

The smoke filled the window and had already backed down to nearly floor level. Usually searching an apartment would require two men, working on their hands and knees, starting at one point along a wall and traversing along the edges in order to not miss closets, doorways, and other rooms. I had lived in one of these apartments many years before and was familiar with their layout. I knew there was one door leading out of the bedroom to a hallway with the bathroom directly across. Still on my hands and knees, I moved toward the doorway. I could hear the activity of the other engine company elsewhere in the apartment as they were knocking down a fully involved kitchen fire. The front entrance door, we learned later, had been nailed shut and secured following a police response the week before. The police had had to kick in the door to deal with a domestic call.

I reached the bedroom door and crossed the hallway. I moved through an open door into the bathroom, still on my hands and knees, and came face to face with two large, white and gray pit bulls, both whining and straining at the chains that connected their choke collars to the doorknob. I had just found the "babies."

My visions of small choking infants were gone, but now I had two big, scary-looking pit bull dogs in front of me, acting like little frightened puppies, willing to accept help from anyone who would offer it. For an instant, I remembered how many of us would chuckle when we heard reports of the family dog or cat being praised for their courage and forethought after waking their owners to warn them of a fire or smoke in the house. "Things would be a lot different of those animals had an opposing thumb," we would say. "All they wanted was somebody to open the door!"

I sat back on my haunches trying to untie or unravel the knotted ball of chain links that surrounded the doorknob. Right then, another firefighter reached the doorway from the interior of the apartment, saw what was happening and called to me as he tapped my shoulder.

"Back off. I'll get it," he said in a muffled voice inside of his air mask.

Once my hand was free, an ax quickly separated the doorknob from the door, freeing the chains.

"Thanks. I'll get these two out of here," I said.

"Head out the back through the kitchen, you can't get out the front," he replied, having already discovered the nailed up door.

The smoke was beginning to thin a bit, so I stood up as I grabbed both chain leashes and moved out of the bathroom and toward the kitchen. The dogs resisted, frightened by the sounds of cabinets and door jams being ripped away in the kitchen as several firefighters were checking for extensions and dousing the final small embers remaining. The air was still hazy with some smoke but mostly steam by the time I reached the kitchen with my two uncooperative canines in tow.

"Coming through, coming through," I hollered through my mask. There was no response from the other firefighters, and I wanted to get these poor dogs out quickly so they could breathe some better air.

This time I yelled, "Pit Bulls, Pit Bulls!"

The small group of firefighters, who just before could not hear me, parted like the Red Sea before Moses providing me enough room to bring a heard of buffalo through.

Once down the stairs and into the parking lot, the Mom and daughter quickly took hold of the chains and relieved me of the "babies". I headed straight for the engine to peel off my air pack, and at least get my coat off so I could begin to cool down.

The fire had begun as a grease fire on the stove, and the firefighters had been able to quickly knock it down. Fire damage spread no further than the kitchen and part of the upper rear stairwell, but the entire apartment suffered either water or smoke damage. Fortunately, there were no injuries.

Clean up operations were underway, so once I had cooled down a bit, I thought I'd check on the Mom, her daughter, and the dogs. I walked over to where they had assembled along with neighbors and relatives at the curb. As I approached, the once trapped dogs, both of which just a half hour earlier were whining and cowering as they needed to be dragged across the floor into the hallway, now lurched toward me as I approached. Snarling and barking, the dogs were being held tight by their owner who now saved me from being ripped to shreds by two aggressive watchdogs that had finally remembered how tough they were.

So much for gratitude, but I figured that once I had done MY job, they could go back to doing theirs.

Fair enough.

Chapter Seven

The Ambulance:
The Early Days

I was assigned to the ambulance almost immediately, as were other recruits at other stations or shifts. It was often a dirty and unpleasant job, and as such was typically assigned to those with the least seniority on shift. We only had Advanced First Aid training, so technical and diagnostic abilities weren't needed that often, and it was still a grab-and-run operation much of the time. We were still in the process of evolving from Advanced First Aid level training, and about a year and a half away from our first steps into Emergency Medical Technician training that was rumored to be available soon.

For the first year and a half on the job I was still pulling the short end of the straw, assigned to ambulance duty andtraining even newer recruits on the ambulance. It actually wasn't that bad.. I'd slowly grown to enjoy ambulance duty because of the variety and excitement it offered each shift day. Part of my initial anxiety about the ambulance was due to my lack of knowledge and the fear that I might hurt someone. With time, and with the additional study and reading, I became more confident and was eager to learn more.

Tom Henshaw had taken the test for the fire department at the same time I did and trailed only a name or two behind me on the eligibility list. So, in less than a year, a couple of retirements brought him and two others to our shift, each of them alternating on the ambulance with me until they came up to speed. I may have been the so-called veteran at the time, but only by a few months. The Captain felt I knew enough about the routines and policies, and I was assigned to train the newboots. It was also another of those jobs delegated to those lowest on the totem pole.

One of Tom's first ambulance calls was to a low income apartment building on our city's northwest side for a report of a woman who had a miscarriage. We assumed this would be a basic transport until we arrived on the scene.

A thin and gaunt looking woman, probably in her 30's, but looking more like 50, was sitting on the toilet in her apartment bathroom with a cigarette in her hand and her sweatpants bunched down around her ankles. "The baby's in there," she said in a deep tobacco voice, pointing down between her legs into the toilet.

"How far along were you," I asked.

"About 5 or 6 months," she replied, slowly blinking as if trying to focus on my face.

Tom and I moved the stretcher to just outside the bathroom door. Together we lifted the woman up and over to the stretcher where we applied thick compresses between her legs along with a couple of towels.

SOP dictated that we'd need to gather up the placenta

and fetus, now floating in a bloody mess in the toilet. We could see a very tiny shoulder and arm along with the back of a tiny head poking up from the wet and bloody slurry. Still a recruit myself, I was a bit shaken by this first-time experience. So much so, I was going to pull what little rank I had and tell Tom to grab some towels and wrap up the toilet contents. Before I could even suggest it, I remembered that his wife was expecting in a couple of months, so he was probably as rattled as I was. I told him to wrap up the mom in some blankets to keep here warm and went back into the bathroom.

Donning plastic gloves didn't help reduce the "yucchh" factor much as I reached down on both sides of the placenta and fetus, pulled them up from the water and let the small load drip a bit before placing it in the middle of a couple of towels laid out on the floor. I folded each corner of the towels over, placing the wrapped up package into yet another towel. As Tom stayed with the patient in the back of the ambulance, I placed the towel covered "package" on the front seat next to me for the trip to the ER.

Once at the hospital, we brought the woman into the ER, explaining the circumstances to the doctor and nurse. Once out of the cubicle, I told the nurse that I had the fetus and placenta from the toilet in the ambulance and would bring it in. She led me to a separate area, directing me to a metal exam table. I placed the towel covered fetus down, again explaining what we had found.

"That's really terrible," said the nurse as we stood on either side of the table. I was wiping off my hands again, while she continued to ask a few questions and enter notes on her clip board.

After a minute or so we heard what sounded like squeaking. "What's that?" I said as we both looked around. Another squeak and we both noticed that the towels were moving.

"Holy shit!", we both said in unison.

We quickly folded back the towels and corners revealing the tiny infant, barely enough to fill your hand, moving its arms and legs with a barely audible squeak. In the flurry of activity that followed, the infant and tissue were gathered up by the nurse and rushed from the cubicle to another area as she barked out orders for assistance and equipment.

A doctor explained to us later that they believed that when the infant hit the cold water, it's need for oxygen was diminished enough so that whatever oxygen it was drawing from the placenta kept it alive without showing any signs of respirations or even a pulse had we even checked. Wrapping it up in the towels, along with a bumpy trip on the seat next to me, was enough to get things active he surmised.

We kept calling the ER for most of the rest of our shift. Unfortunately, due to lack of lung development, the 6 month old fetus died overnight. I don't know about Tom, but I certainly never assumed anything again on an ambulance call. The next two decades would offer reminders that what seems like a DOA (dead on arrival) sometimes might surprise you.

While most ambulance calls before the paramedic program were often a routine transport of someone with chest pains, stroke symptoms, or common injuries such as broken bones, lacerations, and neck injuries, some stood out as both unique and unforgettable. We responded to homes, places of business, traffic accidents, and public falls – involving citizens tripping in municipal or retail areas – in addition to responding to all fire calls to offer quick transport to either civilians or firefighters injured on the scene.

The worst thing I could hear when arriving at the scene of a call usually happened while walking up the sidewalk or stairway. I'd meet a waiting cop or firefighter who relished the opportunity to utter – often with a smile -- a grisly warning.

"You're gonna love this one!" he'd say, maybe rolling his eyes back a bit as he helpfully opened and held the door. Walking into a room without such a warning and seeing something gross is bad enough, but hearing that always magnified the dread-factor by several levels.

This warning often preceded a bad industrial accident, suicide, or other injury causing catastrophic damage to tissue or grotesque rearranging of body parts. Serious and fatal traffic accidents always offered up a bloody variety of ways that a body could be smashed, lacerated, crushed, amputated, or burned.

One of my first fatal traffic accidents involved a woman who was killed instantly when an out-of-control car veered off the street and slammed into her as she was walking on the sidewalk. The car struck a large tree with her caught in between. When we arrived we found the car on top of the now uprooted tree and her body beneath it, split wide open at impact. Once the car was removed by a tow truck and crane, we literally had to pull sections of intestine from several branches, draped like thick holiday tree decorations.

As we gathered more and more organs and tissue, my partner began hollering, "Oh my God, there's a kid here too!". He spotted an entirely separate set of internal organs, only much smaller than the woman's. The entire operation stopped as other firefighters and cops gathered close to the branches to see.

Without saying a word, the Lieutenant reached down and hoisted up a collar and leash, revealing the second victim was actually the victims' dog. Normally a tragic discovery on its own, it was still a relief as we continued recovering body parts.

But the worst calls were finding a body in the summer that had started to decompose. Rarely was any foul play involved. They were usually just people living alone who weren't checked on or weren't missed someplace over a period of several days.

One call involved such a find in a local trailer park in the peak of a long summer stretch of heat and humidity. The body inside had almost started to cook in the increasing and stifling heat inside of the closed up trailer. One firefighter commented that even the flies inside were trying frantically to get out of the closed windows. Both an ambulance and police squad car responded following a report of an awful smell coming from the trailer. As it happened, both the ambulance and the squad car had the benefit of a new recruit riding along that day.

We quickly decided that both of our recruits would have the responsibility of going inside the trailer, dressed in disposable white hooded coveralls and wearing air packs, bagging up the decedent and bringing him out on a stretcher. After all, we joked, what better time to demonstrate professional cooperation between Police and Fire, right?

"Brownie", our recruit, was joined by the brand new female police officer who was also in her first few weeks of training. Both donned their gear, and after receiving instructions on how to bag the body, reluctantly and tentively entered the trailer. As we "veterans" outside exchanged small talk, we could hear the ocassional blurted and muffled "Oh, jeez," or "Gimme a break" from inside. Eventually the two newbies appeared at the door, each at one end of a stretcher with the body all wrapped up in plastic.

It only took a few moments for them to roll the stretcher to the police van that had arrived to transport the body to the County Morgue. Returning toward us, the two recruits had removed their air masks and were finally gulping some unbottled fresh air. The police recruit, immediately after pulling off her face mask, forgot that she still had her gloves on and reached up with one hand and wiped her face where the mask was – even though a micro-second before we had collectively shouted "Nooooooo!" as we saw her hand move toward her face. Realizing what she'd done, she turned pale and nearly fainted. She spent the next ten minutes dousing her face with water from the trailer's garden hose, having learned a valuable lesson.

We were still only a Basic Life Support (BLS) ambulance, and I continued to take an active part in some very small advancements by helping to introduce our own fabricated emergency childbirth kits on each of our three rigs – just a year before such kits became commercially available – and began to carry my own personal tools as well. These included a pair of scissors for cutting through clothing to gain access to injuries along with a fancy new penlite which came in handy to check for pupil dialation, etc. Both were contained in snappy leather holster that I added to my belt with the same pride as if I was Batman with a new utility belt.

The holster was prompted by an earlier, somewhat embarrassing, incident. I was already being ribbed by some co-workers for carrying and using some of these non-invasive diagnostic tools, but found some others were following suit. Once, after responding to a report of a drug overdose, I reached to my shirt pocket to retrieve my penlight to check the patients' pupils. As I hovered over the semi-concious teenager in the back seat of a car, I heard my partner and a couple of guys from the engine company start to smirk. It took me a few seconds to realize that I was frantically clicking away at my ballpoint pen instead. For the rest of the duty shift, I was referred to as "Dr. Bic".

Soon, a few of us even began carrying stethescopes and blood pressure cuffs –some donated by relatives who were nurses or doctors – to gather additional information to pass on to ER physicians, even though some of them didn't trust us enough to take advantage of our information. The Paramedic Program, at least for us, was still a few years away.

I liked working in the ambulance in those early days. It was a constant source of new experiences and offered a degree of relative independence working primarily with one partner. The more calls we experienced, however, contributed toward confirming just how far behind we were to some communities when it came to advanced life support training and capabilities. A handful of us newer firefighters began to push more for taking the next few steps toward upgrading our training and equipment.

Chapter Eight

Emergency Medical Services and the Fire Department

As recruits, Rob Roland and I were assigned to the Red Shift at Station #1 Heaquarters in downtown Des Plaines. The two story, three-bay firehouse was the eastern section of a much larger old brick building. The center of the building was home to City Hall, its offices and associated departments, and the City Council chamber where its regular meetings were held. The Police Department headquarters filled the western section. The station dated back to horse-drawn wagon days. The old folding stable doors were still in place where horses had been housed in stalls at the back of the station. The area was now used as a workshop.

Our bunkroom, dayroom, kitchen and showers were located upstairs at the top of a single straight flight of stairs that emptied down below onto the apparatus floor. The slide pole that used to be located in the corner of the dayroom had been removed years before as larger apparatus encroached on the pole's landing area. The upstairs area for the pole had since been converted to a single stool bathroom.

Station #1 housed Engine 61, Ladder Truck 81, and Ambulance 71 which, at that time, was an old International Truck outfitted with lights and siren, a stretcher, a long bench, and a few cabinets for first aid equipment. Two men were assigned to the ambulance each morning for that shift day. Newboots like Roland and me were immediately assigned to alternately ride along with the assigned crew as helpers and observers. Now that we had our Advanced First Aid cards earned during our few weeks of training, we'd be expected to become part of the normal two-man crew within a week or so. Ambulance duty was never assigned based on training or ability, but rather on seniority – or the lack of it. At the time, this assignment was considered punishment duty for more seasoned firefighters.

There was one other brand new, shiny and untested member of the department that started the same day we came on shift. A brand new 1971 Cadillac Ambulance. It had been designed and built specifically for emergency medical transport, and had more cabinet space strategically placed for access, a new emergency light array, built in suction devices, blood pressure cuff and meter, and new radios. It was also built with considerably more patient area head room to better allow for performing CPR enroute and for hanging IV's -- even though we were still a year or so away from beginning any sort of paramedic training.

The fire department had been directly transporting patients to the hospital for only a couple of years, I learned. Previously an engine company would be dispatched to an emergency medical call, armed only with a first-aid kit and a trusty "Pulmotor" which was an oxygen bottle with a controllable pressure valve along with large and small face masks. The responding engine company would do what they could until an ambulance -- a converted hearse -- was dispatched from a local funeral home. If necessary, the funeral home would transport to nearby Holy Family Hospital ER.

Once at the ER, also pre-dating our modern paramedic service, patients would be evaluated and treated by Doctors who themselves may had been either near retirement, were low on the seniority list, or who just drew the short straw on assignments that week. I learned to be grateful for many of the nurses who regularly worked the ER. Because of their experience in the ER over many years, they could sometimes help avert the ocassional diagnostic disaster.

There were some ER physicians who stood out as competent, alert, and dedicated to emergency medicine, but they were the younger minority that eventually helped established emergency medicine as a speciality. For the time being, it seemed, the emergency room was sometimes just as scary as our ambulances were, manned by first-aid trained rookies. At least with a spanking new Cadillac, we could get to the hospital much faster.

My first ambulance call was the maiden voyage for our Cadillac as well.

The Klaxon horn blasted followed by "Code One. Maryville Academy, possible overdose on the ball field off of Golf Road." We knew where that was. The one-time orphanage now housed hundreds of troubled or abused kids of all ages. We could expect at least two to three calls a month there between pulled false alarms, overdoses, and small trash fires.

I had to ride in the back of the ambulance as Dan Willis and Dave Perry sat in front. Willis was senior to me by less than a year, but was experienced enough to enjoy having a newboots on board, and Perry had only a few years left until retirement. Dave never seemed to get excited about anything and was a calming influence whenever things got crazy.

Arriving on the scene, we found a 13 year old boy being held on the ground by three grown men; each one of them were alternately being lifted off the ground as the boy fought with them. His long, shoulder length hair was tangled and partially covered his bright red face. Sweat was pouring off of him. As we approached, the boy's eyes nearly popped out his head. He looked straight at me and screamed something about dragons and fire.

It was a struggle, but six grown men averaging 180 to 200 pounds finally got the kid strapped down on a stretcher which we slid into the ambulance and secured. I was practically sitting on his chest holding his wrists when everyone left. Two coaches and a priest left us and returned to the ball field while Willis and Perry took their seats in the front of the ambulance. "Hold him down, and don't let him bite you!" Perry said as we left, lights and siren blaring, for the hospital.

LSD was still popular at the time, and since the teenager seemed to think he was a fire breathing dragon being held against his will, we made the assumption that he more than likely was having a bad trip on our dime, so to speak. Lacking any proper leather restraints, we had wrapped him tightly in two blankets that I learned was the restraint of choice in most cases and usually very effective. In this case, our passenger's arms were now free, and I was forced to sit on his chest restraining his arms while holding tight to a handful of sweat soaked hair to keep him from biting me. We fought all the way to the hospital.

My two senior instructors and I, along with the help of one of the hospital's male orderlies and a security guard, finally extracted the combative teen from the ambulance and transferred him to an ER gurney with proper restraints. Once totally tied down, I looked around to find my two mentors nowhere in sight.

My shirt was torn in the front where the pocket had pulled away from the rest of the shirt, and I was drenched in sweat, with my hair so wet it looked like I'd just stepped out of a shower - were it not for the grass stains on my elbows and forearm. I returned to the ER loading dock to find my two partners, relatively dry and clean, leaning against the back of the ambulance waiting for me. "So what do think about ambulance duty," said Perry, now that I'd had my first call.

"Are they all like this?" was all I could say. I soon learned that some could actually be worse.

In the early 70's, ambulance calls were just that... an ambulance call. Who provided the service varied from one part of the country to the other. In addition to fire departments, hospitals, funeral homes, or one of many privately owned ambulance services could dispatch ambulances. They were basically transport services, not intended for serious or intensive treatment on the scene but rather for rapid transport to a medical facility.

The variety of calls ranged everywhere from small injuries to massive catastrophes but the level of treatment didn't vary that much. Bandage, splint, offer oxygen, and get'm on a stretcher was the main SOP. That routine was just starting to change.

"We don't need any paramedic program"

Our department's evolution from a basic first-aid ambulance with stretcher and oxygen tank to fully trained paramedics manning a Mobilie Intensive Care Unit (MICU) initially was championed by both younger line firefighters and progressive ER doctors and others. It could be argued, however, that our department's evolution was primarily due to two guys named Gage and Desoto.

Gage and DeSoto weren't on our department though. They were two characters on a popular TV show in the early 1970's called "Emergency". They, along with two ER doctors and an attractive nurse at the fictional "Rampart General Hospital," teamed up each week to save a variety of lives using the lifesaving equipment on board Rescue Truck 51.

The then new and experimental paramedic program was already in place in the Los Angeles area and provided fodder for the new TV series. For many of us still at the first aid level, the concept of firefighters giving enhanced emergency treatment in the field under the direction of a physician on the radio was a source of continual frustration. As our Hollywood counterparts administered life saving drugs, established life sustaining IV's, and even shocked full cardiac arrest patients back to life, we could only offer a whiff of oxygen, a bandage, a splint or – worst case scenario – frantically administered chest compressions and mouth to mouth resuscitation as we sped to the hospital.

We quickly learned that we could do more and that a committment by the city to provide both training and equipment was essential. There were about 4 or 5 of us who kept pushing for the new program, mostly younger post-recruits on the job still full of high hopes and idealism. Our enthusiasm, unfortunately, wasn't shared by either the department administration or city council.

Local city hall opposition was centered around the Mayor's opinion that since we were located close to two major hospitals, "We don't need any paramedic program." True, the hospitals were nearby, but the value of the paramedic program wasn't in short transport time but in stabilizing a patient immediately, on scene, before transport was even considered. Through training, radio telemetry – which remotely transmitted electrocardiograms – and guidance by physicians on the radio, trained paramedics on-site could administer life saving drugs and even "shock" a cardiac arrest victim's heart back into a normal rhythm. Once stablized, with essential drug routes established, the patient could then be transported. Though a common expectation today, in 1971 ambulances were still a "grab and run" operation.

The mind-set locally in the early 70's was understandable as the program was still experimental for many, and merely Hollywood exaggeration to others. Still, a few local champions including both community leaders and visionary physicians pushed hard for local adoption of the program. With a few nearby suburbs already participating in the program, the City of Des Plaines was still holding out.

Most of us younger recruits were manning the ambulances because at the time ambulance duty was still an assignment for whowever was lowest on the shift totem pole. Those of us working the ambulance were keenly aware of the progress made in neighboring communities since we often met up with them at the ER. While we found ourselves sometimes struggling with a non-responsive patient as we performed CPR in the back of our basic life support ambulance enroute to the hospital, once there we saw other crews tending to concious and breathing cardiac patients as they unloaded them – still attached to a monitor by chest leads and an IV – from their fully equipped MICU's. We needed to find a way to get our message across because just complaining wasn't working.

Once, following a particularly frustrating call where I felt that better training, more advanced equipment and physician-supervised patient stabilization may have made a significant difference, I got mad. As soon as I was off shift the next morning, I remembered what our Mayor had said a few weeks before. I grabbed a marker and scribbled, in quotes "Due to our close proximity to two hospitals, I don't feel we need a paramedic program." Since this was an accurate quote from the newspaper, I added the Mayor's name below. At the bottom I drew a rudimentary skull and crossbones. Certainly a bit of youthful overkill, but I was in the grips of a passionate crusade and hadn't learned yet how to keep quiet and reconsider my actions before proceeding

I hung copies of this letter-sized quote wherever I could, including the halls of the City Hall building where our own Fire Station #1 shared space with City administrators and the Police Department. They lasted a day, and I was promptly chastized by our Chief who, unfortunately at the time may have agreed with the Mayor.

My next move was to author an anonymous op-ed letter to the editor of our local weekly newspaper calling for the city to explore the potential of a paramedic program. I began the letter posing a hypothetical situation of a man standing in the middle of a street that was the border between our city and neighboring Mt. Prospect -- a village that had instituted the paramedic program just months earlier. "That man, suffering a cardiac arrest would have a 60 percent better chance of survival," I wrote, "...if he were to fall to the west into Mt. Prospect than if he fell to the east in Des Plaines."

Once we knew that we'd made a serious case for the program, we followed up by encouraging the local paper to do a "man on the street" interview piece asking the question, "Do we need a paramedic program in Des Plaines?" Partly due to previous editorials and comparisons with surrounding communities, it became clear that local taxpayers were wising up.

Others were also pushing for the program, talking to local aldermen and encouraging neighbors and friends to speak up. Once I invited the physician that was training all of the new paramedics and spearheading the new program. Dr. Stanley Zydlo, along with a suburban resident who, championing a massive civic effort, was instrumental in having the program adopted in her community, agreed to attend. Dr. Zydlo brought audio tapes of a few actual emergency calls to representatives of our city council's health committee. City legislators were impressed, but little action was taken.

Eventually we learned that one of the aldermen was married to a nurse. We approached him with the hopes that he'd instigate serious discussion on the council. As a political incentive, we suggested that this could also be a significant opportunity to cast himself as a major proponent of the program in future political campaigns. His wife was a nurse, and she helped both verify and provide additional credibility to our appeals.

Realizing the positive impact of the program on the community and with solid support from his wife, and also reacting to our suggestion that in years to come he could campaign as the "Father of the Paramedic Program," he finally brought the idea before the council. Armed with all the current facts and figures, the program was finally approved.

At that same meeting, the Fire Chief announced his retirement and passed the ball to his successor, a man who began his term as Fire Chief with the task of creating a new paramedic program in our city. He was not very happy with some of us who championed the new program, but soon efficiently and effectively helped lead our department fully into the 20th century.

Our first fully equipped Mobile Intensive Care Network, manned by trained paramedics, went into service in 1974.

Chapter Nine

Bullets and Shootings and Guns

Even with all the new digital special effects tools available these days, Hollywood still can't seem to get blood right. Technicians try hard to get blood the correct color, but the consistency is too thin. They might get the color nearly correct, but then fail to factor in time, which can dramatically change the color of blood from bright red to a dull brown. One special effects team might get the color and the consistency near perfect, but then the mixture proves to be too translucent allowing the floor pattern to show through an otherwise dramatically expanding pool of blood. Karo Syrup and food coloring might be better than ketchup, but only first responders and emergency room staffers know the full spectrum of spilled blood.

Unless they were military veterans with even minimal exposure to combat injuries, many firefighters are initially surprised at their first few calls involving blood loss. A brief visit to the County morgue during training, however instructive the intentions, doesn't prepare most for what they eventually see, smell and deal with after arriving on the scene of a traffic accident or crime scene.

When I was a small boy of 5 or 6, my Dad served as a local Police Reserve officer, mostly helping out directing traffic or at community events and parades. At times he'd ride along in a squad car for a shift. When he'd get home, I'd overhear him recounting events to my Mother, and I'd hear phrases like, "We had to scrape up another accident victim off the highway," or other such colorful terms. For years I would envision rescue workers with large coal shovels scooping up body parts and innards – larger versions of what I'd seen while helping to clean fish – off the neighborhood roads.

Didn't know the gun was loaded!

Gunshot wounds, self-inflicted or not, were surprising both in how severe some were and how severe some weren't. My first ambulance run involving a gunshot wound was an accidental shooting. A middle-aged homeowner discharged a small caliber handgun before cleaning it, wounding himself in his left calf. In my minds' eye, I was expecting to see a massive pool of blood and a family member or two frantically keeping tension on a homemade tourniquet around his leg, as the victim lay screaming and squirming in pain

We were greeted at the door by the man's oldest son, who led us through the living room to the kitchen. Sitting at the kitchen table were a middle aged man, a woman and a teenage girl. One chair was pulled out where the son must have been sitting. Everyone was quiet though a bit apprehensive when we came in, focused more it seemed on the police officer who had preceded us into the room. Looking at the family there at the table, I started to wonder who was the actual shooting victim..

Before we could ask, the woman, obviously the man's wife, judging from the level of disgust in her voice, stood and moved around to the back of the man's chair. "He went and shot himself in the leg," she said as she bent down pointing to his left leg. Someone had taken a scissors or shears and opened the pant leg of his jeans up to the knee. Twisting his leg out to reveal the back of his calf, he pointed out what appeared to be a small puncture wound, bleeding so little that it had barely stained his jeans. A small .22 caliber round had entered high on his calf with no exit wound visible.

Instead of a blood filled crime scene and a panicky family to deal with, we took his vital signs, placed him on a stretcher and transported him to the hospital. His wife rode with us as well, inflicting more verbal shots at him that may have been worse than his gunshot wound. We learned later that the bullet had travelled down through the calf muscle only to lodge under the skin almost at the front of his leg, just above his ankle.

Self-Inflicted: Bad aim, Good aim

The next two gunshot wound calls were more decisive. Each one was a suicide. The first was a despondent man who sat on a chair next to his motel room bed, placed a shotgun into his mouth and fired. In such cases, it was a common practice to call an ambulance crew. In the early days it was to be able to check the box on the police report confirming that medical personnel were called or sometimes to confirm that a victim was either dead or needed immediate transport. Cops usually did not want to make these official determinations, and for good reason.

After the paramedic program was in full operation, the SOP was to confirm death officially through a cardiogram transmitted to the hospital and a confirmation by an ER physician. Sometimes the conditions were more than obvious, but paperwork required that certain boxes get checked.

The fellow in the motel room had done the job more than effectively. He was still sitting upright in a chair, the shotgun laying a few feet in front of him where it landed after an apparently unrestricted recoil. His body was leaning back in the chair. Most of his head was gone, leaving only the neck topped off by what was left of his lower jaw. The rest of his head was literally sprayed up and away from the shoulders in a wide pattern similar to that of a peacock in full display. Bone and tissue fragments, along with tufts of hair still clung to the wall, except where some of the larger or heavier pieces had fallen away and dropped to the floor.

We helped get the victim into a body bag so the cops could transport him to the county morgue. We never learned what had driven him to suicide, but I remember noticing that some of his tissue had landed on a full color framed photo of a man with his family, including a wife and two pre-teen daughters. I could only assume the man in the photo was the victim. We learned later that the victim had previously put a handgun to his head twice and had pulled the trigger, each time failing to score a lethal shot. He finally went out to his car and retrieved the shotgun and returned to his room to finish the job.

The second call proved that what you see isn't always what you get. The paramedic crew from our south station was called early one morning to a motel near the airport where the cleaning crew had discovered an apparent suicide victim in one of the rooms. The police wanted a quick confirmation that he was dead so they could gather up the body for transport. Once again, the box needed to be checked.

As the paramedic crew arrived, they were led into room 112 where an adult male apparently in his 50's lay, still propped up against the headboard by several pillows, with the bed sheet pulled up almost to his neck. Blood trailed down from both a small entrance wound at his left temple, and another slightly larger exit wound at his right temple.

In a perfunctory and routine fashion, the paramedics applied EKG leads to the victim's chest and rib cage prior to plugging the cables into the Lifepak. Once connected, they could run a short section of tape showing no cardiac activity. As one of them reached over the body to connect a pad to the far side of the victim's chest, with his head just inches from the victim's face, the paramedic heard a soft muttering. "I'm cold."

The paramedic recoiled back so quickly that he dropped the cables and fell back on top of the victim's legs before rolling quickly off to stand up, yelling, "Holy Shit! This guys' alive!"

Apparently, when the police arrived and saw the obvious head wound, they had failed to make a closer inspection of the body, which may have revealed a slow, yet short, breathing pattern underneath the sheet that covered his chest. The arriving paramedics, also believing they were there only to confirm a death that in fact had already been confirmed by the police, also failed to notice any slight chest movement before attaching the first lead. A routine confirmation call instantly became an advanced life support emergency.

After completing the EKG leads, they established that there was still a weak and thread pulse. Once an IV was established, the patient was transported to the ER. We learned later that though the man tried in earnest to kill himself, all he accomplished was severing the optic nerves leaving him totally blind for the rest of his life.

The next "gun to the head" suicide attempt I responded to was a more successful attempt, but not without some preliminary excitement and a personal scare.

Parking Lot Scare

Summer nights at the firehouse often found a few of us gathering at the front of the station either on a bench permanently placed between two apparatus bay doors, or on a variety of lawn chairs or office chairs drafted for our evening discussions out front. It was a time for department gossip, union gripes, politics and whatever subject surfaced. We became magnets for people passing by to drive up and ask for directions, and it certainly did little to enhance our image among the public, but I will admit these were some of the most enjoyable times spent on duty.

My older brother Bob, a patrolman with the police department, was patrolling one warm, summer evening in our district. He had stopped by the fire station after seeing a few of us gathered out front. We chatted for bit, then he continued on, saying he needed to pick up some paperwork at the hospital, located just a couple of miles north of our station.

So it's understandable that I may have over reacted to the call that came in over the klaxon about 10 minutes later. "Code One, Holy Family Hospital, north parking lot. Gun shot wound, police on the scene." I was assigned to the ambulance that day, so it was only a few short steps to Ambulance 71, a still shiny new Cadillac. Don Simmons, my partner on the ambulance that day, was among the group out front and quickly slid into the passenger seat as I claimed the driver's side without discussion. Taking a right hand turn while still accelerating, I'm positive that we completed part of the turn on two wheels, and then I floored it.

As we approached the solo flashing light on a squad car at the northern end of the parking lot, we saw it was placed just behind another sedan with the driver's side door wide open. Relief flushed over me like a cold shower right after a sauna when I saw Bob standing there waving his clipboard over his head as we drove up.

"Guy just pulled in and must have popped himself in the head," he said. "I think he's still breathing,"

My brother was his usual calm, controlled and stoic self. He had a well-known quiet confidence and control that was often contagious enough to settle down most everyone nearby, earning him in years to come the respectful nickname "Obi-Wan". The sight of the bloodied driver sitting behind the steering wheel with Bob standing nearby reminded me of an early traffic stop Bob had experienced years before while still new on the job himself.

After pulling over a speeder doing over 60 in a 45mph zone, Bob had approached the vehicle from the side as usual, moving to the driver's side window and politely asking for the driver's license and registration. Still somewhat new on the job, he failed to see the driver concealing the movement of his right hand. The driver pulled out a gun and then quickly moved it across his chest from right to left. His intention was to point the gun straight at Bob who was standing to the left of the driver and slightly behind his left shoulder. As he moved the gun up and to the left, the muzzle caught in between two buttons on his shirt. Apparently, when he attempted to jerk his gun free, the driver squeezed the trigger and fired a .38 caliber round directly into his own heart, killing himself instantly.

Here in the hospital parking lot, Bob had already removed a revolver from the man's right hand. The driver's side window had been shattered either by a bullet or Bob's nightstick making entry to the car. The driver had shot himself in the right side of the head, and the large caliber round left a larger exit wound on the other side. Blood and tissue was spattered on the inside of the door, and a vast amount of blood had already soaked the top of his jacket and shirt. Leaning closer, I heard a small gurgle.

Don already had our stretcher out of the ambulance and next to the car. Since the head wound was so severe, we passed up our usual SOP's and quickly pulled him from the car and onto the stretcher. I pulled him forward slightly, enough to get my arms behind him and under his left and right armpit. Pulling up and out, as Don grabbed his legs, the victim's head rolled first left then right on my chest, covering my uniform shirt in blood and tissue.

We practically threw him onto the stretcher, and when he was quickly belted in, I grabbed a plastic esophageal airway and inserted it into his throat, first with the tip pointing up, sliding along the roof of his mouth, then turning 90 degrees to rest in place, hopefully helping to provide a more clear airway. We jammed the stretcher into the ambulance, slammed the door, and while Dave drove, I radioed dispatch to advise the ER we were coming in from their parking lot with a gunshot wound to the head.

It was a quick drive from the north lot to the ambulance bay, and we were met by a couple of orderlies, a nurse and two hospital security officers. Normally we'd wheel the stretcher into the ER, but there was a gurney waiting for us on the dock, making the transfer perhaps a little less clinical, but much faster. The victim quickly disappeared into the ER and behind some curtains. Within minutes he was pronounced dead. Apparently, the gurgling was the sound of some air being released from the lungs. He was most likely dead before we even arrived in the parking lot.

My shirt was soaked in blood and I found a sink near the ER to wash off my hands and try to clean tissue off my shirt. Another police officer popped his head in to tell us that the patient had just murdered his own family in another community a few hours earlier, and the officer cynically observed that the man apparently saved the state plenty of money by doing himself in. With that information, any sense of solemnity or sadness quickly changed to a much less sympathetic aftermath. The blood all over my uniform now seemed even more offensive than before.

As I was cleaning off my shirt, I reached into my left pocket to remove a small pad of paper I kept for notes. It was full of blood and had a couple of small clumps of brain matter attached.

Holding it briefly for the cop to see, I said, "Well, these must be his piano lessons," and then placed the note pad into the bio-waste bag.

Dangerous Donuts

Shootings with police involved always increase both apprehension and imagination. Responding to a report of a shooting, police on the scene, man down could mean a lot of differing things. Without further information, we'd usually drive a bit faster than normal if it was possible that a cop was the victim.

On one such call we pulled up to a 7-11 Store located on our eastern border with a neighboring Township and met a County Sheriff's officer. He stood holding open the front door whose upper glass panel sported a bullet hole at the center of radiating shattered glass still held in place by a plastic inner layer.

The shooting victim was on the floor just inside, sitting up with his right hand holding a fist full of paper towels soaked in blood. Only when we noticed that his left hand was handcuffed to the leg of a shelving unit did we realize the victim was the armed robber himself.

We found an entry wound on the right side of his neck near the back and an exit wound also near the back of his neck but on the left side. A bullet had broken the skin on the right, then traveled through relatively unrestricted flesh immediately under the skin for a couple of inches before exiting. There was plenty of blood, but it did not appear that any arteries had been affected – a stroke of luck for this would-be robber, considering the close proximity to the carotid arteries feeding his brain. (Or in this case, perhaps a reasonable facsimile of one.)

The County officer had pulled up in front of the store just a moment or two before the robbery began and was totally unaware, as was the store clerk, that a robbery was about to begin.

As the robber was bringing his sawed off shotgun up from under his coat and was about to push in close into the face of the surprised store clerk, the officer spotted the gun while still outside the store as he was exiting his squad car. Fearing that the next image he'd see would be a shotgun blast, the officer drew his pistol in a reflex action, took aim and fired a shot through the glass front door. He had taken aim for center mass as trained, but the glass deflected the bullet, giving it a slight upward and skewed trajectory directing it quickly in and out of the thief's neck. The surprised gunman spun slightly to the right, dropped his shotgun and fainted, dropping like a wet rag.

We applied some new dressings and transported the now conscious but somewhat panicky desperado to the hospital with another County officer sitting in back as well. The robber survived with relatively minor injuries, and the officer eventually was disciplined for his actions. He had not taken into consideration that there were other patrons in the store who could have been injured or killed by his reflex action.

Ironically, the only civilian injury resulting from the incident was a broken tooth, suffered two days later when a senior citizen customer from the same store bit into a doughnut with a 9 mm round inside.

FAA Shooting

Our department's paramedic program had just been officially implemented in 1974, but with new paramedics still in training, there were only enough qualified graduates to man one MICU housed at our headquarters, Station #1. The other two stations still responded with basic life support (BLS) ambulances, with the advanced life support (ALS) unit called if needed.

Dick Simpson and I were manning Ambulance 72, a BLS ambulance, out of our south side station #2 when we were dispatched on a call for a possible shooting at the local FAA offices located on our city's far southern border. The address was in one of the several office buildings that surrounded a large tollway lake just off Interstate-94, and was placed about as far away as you can go from the complex's southern entrance off of Touhy Avenue. Even with our fast Cadillac ambulance, it took a few minutes to reach the complex and then navigate through the parking lots that surrounded the lake and each building.

As we were approaching the FAA building, the voice on the radio advised us that police were on the scene, at least one victim was down, and the shooter had not yet been taken into custody. Pulling up to the building itself, it looked like a mutual aid SWAT training exercise. Not only were there Des Plaines squads all around, but we literally had to thread our way through and around County PD, State PD and even neighboring Rosemont PD squad cars.

Simpson and I had pulled out the stretcher, and as was the routine, piled up our first aid kit and other cases on top to limit or eliminate any trips back to the ambulance for something we'd forgotten. As we carried the stretcher up a few steps up and into the front entryway, we started down a hallway. The first officer we spied was standing next to a pillar, his gun drawn and held with both hands as he kept it pointed toward the ceiling.

"So where is he?" I asked as we passed, since we still had no idea where the victim was located.

"He's up on the landing between the first and second floor," the cop quickly yelled back.

"Ok, thanks," I replied still moving down the center of the hall.

We passed a couple more pillars before taking a quick left at the end of the hall, and probably should have questioned why each pillar also had an officer -- with gun drawn --

standing alongside. Perhaps they figured we knew something they didn't, but none of them tried to stop us. We soon realized they weren't standing next to the pillars, they were hiding behind them.

Simpson and I made the left turn at the end of the hall, finding the lower section of a two flight, open stairway leading to the floor above.

"He's up there, up there," said another cop, in the same two-hands-on-a-gun-pointing-up posture, against the wall, when we turned the corner.

As we started up the open, two level stairway with our first aid kit and other cases in hand, we came to the first landing and found a well-dressed but disheveled, middle-aged man standing on next to another man laying in the corner in the midst of the broken pieces of a decorative flower vase. The man standing up looked up at us as if we were crazy, then raised his right hand and pointed a large automatic pistol toward us, stopping us cold.

Neither Simpson or I were gun experts, and we failed to notice that the weapon had in fact jammed. The next round – which easily may have been intended for us - hadn't completed its automatic feed into the barrel and was preventing the slide from successfully cycling after his previous shot. We only saw the barrel pointed at us, and not the open slide. Realizing the weapon was jammed, the man stopped repeatedly squeezing the now frozen trigger and lowered it slightly, reaching up with his other hand.

The next thing I noticed was a blur of blue as officers from the top of the next short flight of stairs seemed to fly over our heads -- two or three of them hitting the shooter like linebackers. The tangled mess of bodies tipped and crashed with a thud against the wall behind the gunman. They quickly cuffed him, as Simpson and I moved past to check the victim in the corner.

The victim's breathing was clear and he was conscious. Even though he had obvious wounds in the neck and face, none of the blood was interfering with his breathing, nor was he showing signs of any great external blood loss. We quickly surveyed the rest of his body, finding what appeared to be an entry wound high on his chest and two other wounds. One or more of them could have been an exit wound, or both could have been caused by the sharp edges of the broken vase he had fallen on.

Our quick initial check of his life signs revealed no difficulty in breathing and a strong healthy pulse. Before we could get a blood pressure cuff and stethoscope out of the bag, someone came down the second flight of stairs behind us yelling, "There's another one upstairs! He got shot in the chest!"

MICU 71 hadn't arrived yet, coming from the far north end of the city, and because the victim on the floor was now even talking to us and still had good color, I pulled out a half dozen compresses and bandages out of our kit and dropped them on the floor with Simpson. Grabbing the portable radio and first aid kit, I told him to start bandaging this patient up and that I'd check out the one upstairs.

Up the stairs and down a very short hallway to the left was the FAA main office. A desk and a couple of side chairs were pushed aside or overturned, and the contents of a wastebasket were spilled around, apparently part of the path taken by our fleeing victim on the stairway. A group of shaken office workers were gathered in a small, tight group near a wall. In the center of the main aisle, a large, barrel chested male was on his back on the floor, laying in a spreading pool of blood and surrounded by a couple of other executives. One identified himself as a Flight Surgeon and kept repeating, "He's got a chest wound and he's not breathing," he said more than once. "He needs to be defibrillated," he added a few times as well. This event was obviously not like the predictable and clinical experiences he was used to.

This victim had been shot point blank in the chest, apparently after the shooter learned he was being laid off. He had no pulse, his pupils were dilated and fixed and his respirations were obviously lacking as both his wide open mouth and nostrils were filled with blood. Later we learned that a single round had obliterated his aortic arch. He was probably dead before he hit the floor.

The flight surgeon kept calling for additional life saving measures, despite my assurances that they would be in vain. Normally I would have directed the incoming paramedic unit to the victim on the stairs, and Simpson and I would have either transported the deceased victim, or remained to assist if the PD decided to transport the body to the county morgue. SOP dictated, however, that EMT's or paramedics were to follow the directions of any MD on the scene.

I grabbed the portable radio and directed the arriving crew on #71 to the second floor -- as directed by a physician on scene. Then, after explaining to the doctor that we had another patient on the stairwell, I left him to watch for the paramedics as they arrived.

Simpson had already bandaged the victim's wounds, and he and I assisted him onto a stretcher and headed for our ambulance parked out front. Hank Friendly and Jerry

Coorzine, the paramedics on #71, passed us in the hall in the opposite direction with all their gear in tow.

"Yours is upstairs with a flight surgeon, " I advised them. "The doc wants someone to intubate and zap him, but he's already cold. You're gonna have to deal with him. I couldn't." Hank and Jerry were clearly miffed that their hard-earned new skills may only be drawn upon to confirm a "triple zero", a term meaning no respirations, no blood pressure and no pulse, and possibly a straight line EKG if requested by the hospital.

We were lucky this time, in spite of having our new, yet still untested, official protocols circumvented by a non-emergency MD. X-rays of our stairwell patient at the hospital later revealed that one bullet had struck him in his chest as he was running from his assailant. In mid-air, the bullet entered his chest, skimmed along his sternum, left the body from the neck and re-entered under his jaw. The bullet finally exited through the face near the nose after passing through his pallet. No vital arteries were affected.

Fortunately, the ability to fully man our other two MICU's with fully trained and equipped paramedics was not that far off.

Chapter Ten

"Run Away" Room

One of the scariest things for firefighters is not being familiar with the environment they are about to enter. Firefighters are trained and experienced in how to deal with superheated, toxic, and poisonous gases, and they are well equipped to deal with many different types of structural or physical hazards. Firefighters don't actually run into burning buildings as often portrayed. Usually they crawl or advance on their hands and knees, depending on the amount of heat and smoke, and knowing the toxic atmosphere a foot or so above their heads can approach 1,000 degrees or more.

The biggest and most common challenge is that firefighters making an intial entry or attack are essentially blind due to heavy smoke. In most situations, they also aren't familiar with the interior room layout, furniture or equipment placement and can't even see where the windows are. Navigating becomes a touch and feel progression into an unknown environment where floors can disappear or ceilings collapse without warning.

Firefighters train to deal with most of these unknowns. For example, they are trained to search for victims by moving in pairs along the interior walls within a structure. Two firefighters, searching for occupants or victims in a building totally charged with smoke from ceiling to the floor, will pick a direction and begin crawling along the floor, one firefighter with one hand on a wall, the other firefighter alongside -- perhaps even at arm's length -- toward the center of the room. Together they advance along the wall, sweeping in front and to the side with their arms or tools, searching for anything.

Reaching a doorway or passage in the wall, they continue along the wall into the room, closet or whatever, searching as they go, checking under beds, around furniture, through closets and more. I learned quickly that when blinded by smoke, a dead cat feels just like a human arm, at least for a few agonizing seconds.

Another way to reduce the hazard of working blind, especially in commercial buildings, is pre-planning and touring buildings and facilities beforehand. This isn't practical for most homes, of course, but is important if the community is home to businesses, industry, and warehousing. Such buildings are easier for fire companies to inspect or tour during a duty day, identifying entries and exits, hazardous materials, unique structural floor plans, and more. Some departments keep information on many local businesses, stores, or plants accessible in the engine for fire officers to consult when responding. The large three-ring notebooks of the early 70's, I'm sure, have long been replaced by a computer data base accessible from a laptop in many responding vehicles

Once such tour was especially helpful to me at one major downtown fire in 1979, involving our historic old movie theatre. The old movie house, at one time host to nationally renowned Vaudeville acts and entertainers, was burning along with a couple of adjacent stores. This became a major fire, requiring the return of all off duty firefighters and the assistance of several neighboring communities. It was the suburban equivalent of a major city's "4 alarm fire".

I was off duty that day and responded to a pager call, as did several other firefighters, from a nearby bowling alley. We had been in the midst of a local firefighters' bowling tournament. We quickly drove to our stations, grabbed our gear, and manned a spare engine to respond downtown. The huge header of smoke just blocks away kept prompted an additional jolt of adrenaline.

As we arrived, the shift captain was coming out of the front entrance of the theater with his body drawing a trailing tail of smoke behind him as he moved. The fire had originated somewhere in the basement of a neighboring store but quickly transmitted up through fake walls and open channels to the second floor which was by now fully engulfed in flames. Firefighters manned large exterior handlines that were piercing the smoke and flames with water streams, and our ladder trucks' main ladder was extended over the building directing even more water from a large nozzle attached to the top rung. Others were training lines from the rear of the building or trying to gain access, as next door communities were responding to calls for mutual aid. The Captain directed several of us to don our masks and make our way down a small wooden stairwell behind the popcorn counter. We were to see if we could check for any spread of flames laterally below the theater lobby through a common cellar area.

Built back in the early 1920's, the wooden stairs were very old, and very dry. We reached the basement, finding flames still under the adjacent jewelry store to the east of the theater, and beginning to extend over our heads along the low ceiling. Then we heard wood cracking. After knocking down the relatively small amount of flames at that point, we began moving back toward the stairs. Before we could make an exit, much of the stairway collapsed. Our path to the outside was gone.

A couple of us had been in this basement just a month before in response to a problem with furnace which resulted in smoke backing up into the building, so we knew that some of the cellars for the theater and adjacent stores may have been connected.

Unable to retreat the way we had come, our only choice was to move in the other direction, hoping there was a way up from the neighboring drug store. As we moved toward the west wall of the theater cellar, we confronted a wall that not only seemed to be closer than I had expected, but blocked any escape to a way up and out.

Huge volumes of water from multiple hoselines outside had filled the entire cellar with water about knee-deep when we first came down. Now, with no apparent way out, the water level had risen dramatically to nearly waist high. Boxes and pressurized cylinders from the soda dispensers were floating around us. The extremely cold water had already filled our boots, and the three of us, armed with only an axe, a two and a half inch hose line and a couple of flashlights, looked at each other and wondered if this was how we were going be found -- three bodies uncovered after pumping out the cellar the following day. To make matters worse, smoke was also stacking up at the ceiling and working down toward our heads.

Strangely, instead of the expected panic one might feel at that point -- a luxury that most firefighters must learn to control -- I had a quick mental replay of the garbage dump scene from the original Star Wars movie when the film's heroes were splashing around in debris laden water while some scary creature slithered around below them.

As I looked at the barrier which became the west wall of a potential watery prison, I remembered an earlier tour of the building and what we had seen in the room with the incinerator. "One of the old fire protection devices that still remain in this room," the building owner explained at the time, "is this sliding metal fire door."

Usually recessed into the wall was a large metal door that was designed to close off the furnace area should there be a fire. The door was usually held in place by a fusible link that would melt at a predetermined temperature and allow gravity to pull the sliding door along a track until closed. For several years, the door had been closed offering a separation between two cellar areas.

"Hey guys, give a hand!" I yelled as we hit the metal wall and began pushing to the right.

The door slowly slid along its rollers to the side and back into the wall, allowing each of us to move into the next cellar, climb the drugstore stairs, and escape into the street through the now broken storefront window.

When fighting any interior fire, whether in a small residential unit or a large factory, firefighters try to be aware of potential escape routes should the need arise. I always called this my "run away room". One of the scariest sounds for any firefighter, amidst the crashing, splashing, and other indistinguishable sounds of any interior firefighting attack, is the call to evacuate. These are usually muffled through air masks but the tone is very clear even if the words are not. Someone yelling "Get the @#&% outa here!" through their air mask a is a real attention grabber.

This time there was no yelling, but a quick recollection of an otherwise boring building tour. Had we not known about the existence of that door, it could have easily been just one wall of a deathtrap. Instead, it became a doorway back out to safety. I always paid extra close attention to any building tours we made from then on.

Chapter Eleven

Running Hot and Cold

Firefighting is enough of a challenge even under ideal or what might be called "normal" conditions. Add the extremes of steamy hot or sub-zero weather and new concerns need to be dealt with. Mix in a blinding snowstorm, damaging winds, or flooding rains and a timely response to a routine automatic trouble alarm is no longer guaranteed.

As a suburb of Chicago, Des Plaines enjoyed both weather extremes. Oppresive heat and humidity in the summer was balanced only a few months later by numbing cold and blizzards. As a result, we could never fully acclimate to either season. Seasoned firefighters in Tuscon, Arizona, may share a condescending giggle with those serving in Nome, Alaska, as I describe our temperature extremes.

HOT

Firefighting gear is considered protective apparel, but coupled with a heatwave driving the thermometer into the

100's, the gear itself can become a hazard. The new space age fire resistive and super insulated coats and trousers also keep heat in, interferring with the body's own cooling system.

I experienced this for the first time when I was much younger and in much better shape than I am in now, but I succumbed because I was unable to recognize the symtoms, and the officer in charge failed to recognize them as well.

It was a 90+ degree August afternoon when we responded to a report of a house fire. Upon arrival we found a three story tenement house with smoke coming out of the first and second floors. All occupants were out and accounted for, so search and rescue didn't provide a sense of urgency, but the close proximity of similar old wooden buildings on either side offered us two prime and vulnerable exposures that needed to be protected.

I was part of a small three-man ladder company -- under manned as was often the case in those days. Our usual manning was at least four, including a driver-engineer, company officer and two firefighters. We were told, along with a crew from the second-in engine, to ladder the building and open up the roof for ventilation. Other crews were already setting up lines for exposure protection, while another crew made an unsuccessful attempt to enter the building with a line through the front door.

Our crew succeeded in laddering the side of the three story building with a 45 foot extension ladder. John Strom and I climbed to the gutter line holding onto the ladder rungs with our left hands and each grasping one of two ends of a 12 foot roof ladder in our right hands. Once at the top, I guided the ladder onto the roof as Strom continued up the ladder behind me also pushing the roof ladder forward.

A roof ladder is a single extension ladder that can be 12 or 14 feet long or longer and is equipped with a folding hook at the top of each rung. The hook can be turned and locked in at a right angle to the ladder in order to secure the ladder over the peak of a roofline. The ladder is then laid flat against the roof offering a working area for firefighters.

I was at the lower edge of the roof at the gutter line and had to push the roof ladder -- hooks deployed -- up and away from me three or four times before the hooks reached the peak, more than 12 feet away, and held tight. Now, each with a fire ax or a pike pole slid into our truckman's belts, we needed to climb this ladder and open up the roof, allowing superheated smoke and air to be released and allow an interior attack. In order to climb the roof ladder, we each had to stand precariously on the upper rung of our ground ladder and literally fall forward on the roof with our arms extended to grasp the bottom rung of the roof ladder.

By this time, I was drenched inside my turnout gear. And the continuing adrenalin jolts triggered by our precarious position over three stories up may have masked some of my usual self-preservation judgement. Sawyer and I took turns with the axe opening up a hole. One of us would stand on the rungs of the roof ladder, while the other would lay down on the ladder gripping a rung with one hand, and holding fast the other firefighter's truckman's belt with the other. In this way we hoped to prevent a crippling if not deadly fall down the roof and to the ground.

With a roughly four foot by four foot hole open, we used the pike pole to jab down toward the ceiling below, attempting to break through to the now smoke charged third floor. At the other end of the roof, flames were licking up under the roofline peak, meaning that we had better move fast or get down.

The ax slipped from my hand, and I felt dizzy. Others had joined us on the roof. The fresher crew that had come up from the other side of the building had brought a Quickie saw, which would make short work of opening other larger holes allowing for greater ventilation. I worked my way down, slipping once or twice, but fortunately only when I also had a firm grip on at least one ladder rung.

Once on the ground, I remember someone telling me to get some water and cool off.

This was easily a decade before the fire service made it SOP to regularly relieve firefighters on the scene. It has since become an accepted practice to allow them to rest and recover -- even if only for a 10 or 15 minute period -- as part of a required and supervised "rehab" location at the fire scene. That was not the protocol today, however. The shift commander at the scene, catching sight of me with my head under an open engine port spewed out a profanity-laced command to get my "ass back up to the roof."

Even though I could be an insubordinate SOB when I wanted to, my judgment was still off just enough to quietly acquiesce and return to the foot of the ladder. I tried a couple of times to get my boot up onto one of the rungs.

My next recollection was bouncing around on the stretcher in the back of Ambulance 71. My coat was off, and I felt ice cold wet towels in my armpits and over my head.

At the hospital ER, as I drifted in and out of diminishing waves of dizziness, two fluid replenishing IV's were started, one in each arm. Soon the room came into focus and thinking became less of a chore. I just had my first experience with heat exhaustion, which I'm told was well on the way toward full blown heat stroke.

The Captain stood at the right side of my gurney with my helmet in his hands. He had picked it up at the scene when he saw me being placed into the ambulance and then speeding away.

"You make sure you get some rest and follow what they tell you," he said as he placed the helmet down on the table at the foot of the gurney, and avoiding direct eye contact. "I was told by others that you had just come down as part of the first response crew ventilating the roof. I probably shouldn't have sent you back, but it's good you never made it back up."

"I don't remember a thing after coming off the ladder," I assured him, enjoying his contrition a bit. "Things got a little hairy with the truck running short."

I just had to add the little dig at the end, but appreciated that he had made the effort to stop by and check.

A few years later, we experienced an historic and record breaking heat wave that gripped the Chicago area, sending hundreds to the hospital, and to the Cook County morgue.

By this time, fire scene rehab practices were the norm, and individual departments took a variety of actions to cope. Independent of department SOP's, our local crews began carrying extra water supplies, five gallon thermos containers filled with ice water each morning, and the department had already allowed for lighter and cooler uniform polo shirts instead of the long or short sleeve uniform shirts and required t-shirts.

Some of those precautions paid off when my engine

company responded to a local nine-story senior citizen housing facility for a report of a possible fire on the top floor. At the time, my own mother lived on the 7th floor. As we pulled up, no smoke was showing, and no other indication of a fire was visible. We'd have to go upstairs ourselves to investigate.

We entered the building lobby, now half filled with seniors wandering about, and no power to the elevators or anything else. The air was still and humid, but laced with all the varied odors you would expect from a large crowd of octegenarians and others in close quarters. Some had just walked down several floors in an even more closed in and isolated stairwell, and anxiously moved to breath in some fresh air coming in through the lobby door. A fire alarm buzzer, obviously battery controlled, blasted throughout the lobby, making it hard for everyone to hear questions or instructions. The only light, other than what came through the front lobby, was supplied by a few emergency lights in the hallways.

Three of us began our trek up the stairs, with our pre-rolled collection of hoselines and nozzle – called a stairwell pack -- in tow as we climbed toward the 9th floor. A few seniors were still slowly making their way down the stairs, with others peering into the stairwell from the doorways as we climbed higher. No one noted any smoke, but we heard on our radio that a passerby had noticed flickering in one of the ninth floor rooms, located just off the stairwell we were climbing. We kept climbing the stairs. 6th floor, 7th floor, 8th floor.

At the 9th floor we were met by a group of seniors who stayed put, each asking what they should do, what was the matter, can anyone shut off the alarm, and so forth. We quickly entered the room at the end of the hall, facing south, where the flickering had been seen. Throughout the entire apartment there were candles blazing. There must have been fifty candles, all lit by the resident.

"I didn't know when the power would come back on so I lit some candles," explained the perplexed 88 year-old lady as fully equipped firefighters entered her apartment.

After helping her blow out most of the candles, leaving a couple burning at the sink, we made our way down. I took a spare radio and stopped off at the 7th floor to check on Mom. As I entered the hallway from the stairwell, each senior lady I passed in the hall said, "Oh, you must be Myrtle's son!" Down the hall stood Mom, looking hot and a bit sweaty from the heat, beaming as only a proud Mom could do as I walked through the hallway in full gear. After a few minutes meeting several of her 7th floor cronies, and assured she was okay, I completed the trip down and back to the engine.

Several of us remained for another hour or so, helping more seniors down and out of the building which was quickly becoming a steam box. Some crews made the nine story trek more than once, having to carry a few elderly residents down the stairs cradled in special chair stretchers. By taking turns, cooling off and keeping hydrated, not one of us succumbed to any heat related difficulties.

COLD

Sub zero weather does more than slow things down. Not all departments have to deal with the severe winters of the northern US, but those that do have set up routines and procedures to try and overcome them. All the planning and preparation, however, sometimes still leaves department personnel and resources unable to cope.

The first obvious challenge in cold weather is that

water freezes. Typical fireground operations often involve a "master stream" or two, delivering high volumes of water into an industrial or large structural fire from the outside. As accurate as engine operators may be in calculating the hydraulics involved, such as friction loss, length of hose, elevation considerations, and nozzle type, most fireground streams can be only so efficient. Once out of the nozzle, the streams begin to break up at varying degrees creating a lot of water droplets and mist. In warmer temperatures, what doesn't evaporate is deposited liberally on everything nearby. That's one of the reasons fire helmets are designed with the long lip at the rear. It keeps water -- as well has an errant hot ember -- from finding its way down the back of a firefighter's neck.

In freezing weather this othetwise minor irritant becomes more than just another hazard to firefighters. When it freezes it can be a serious impediment to firefighting operations overall.

We learned during one particularly cold winter season that when temperatures get to a certain low point, and are sustained there for a day, even the small amount water remaining within the fire engine pumps can freeze, rendering hydrants and the 500 gallons of water carried on the engine totally useless and unattainable. As a result all engine pumps would need to be drained of any water that would be susceptible to freezing and interfering with the ability to pump any water. This meant a moment or two on a fire scene priming the dry pump for operation, but the slight delay was better than the alternative.

In some subzero responses, many joked that the colder it was, the more firefighters wanted to be inside fighting the fire. It was the best source of heat, and it followed that some kidded about not knocking a fire down too fast so they could ward off the cold a bit longer. Even if that were true, it wouldn't let anyone escape the grueling task of sub-zero post-fire cleanup, gathering frozen hose and equipment while slipping on icy surfaces everywhere.

In warm weather, drained fire hoses could be disconnected and rolled up for transport back to the station. In sub-zero weather, the spaghetti-like pattern of hoses surrounding a fire scene is quickly frozen. Much of the water remaining inside freezes and hinders any attempt to drain the rest, and nearly a half-inch of now frozen mist encases the outside of the hose. What normally would be a quick job of rolling up lengths of drained hose instead became an exercise in folding awkward lengths of frozen stiff and heavy hose and heaving them into a department squad or pickup truck bed or other department vehicle for transport. Once back at the station, they would need to be thawed first, then drained and cleaned.

Many firefighters outside during firefighting operation are subject to this frozen spray as well. In addition to icicles forming on helmet rims -- and even from mustaches on those so equipped -- ice formed on the outside of bunker coats and pants, sometimes so thick that it seriously hindered movement.

At one such fire, a Salvation Army truck was on hand providing hot coffee or hot chocolate along with warm cotton gloves to freezing firefighters. When another firefighter and I stopped by to grab a cup to warm up, I reached out and picked up a styrofoam cup full of hot coffee, only to discover that enough ice had formed on my bunker coat and sleeves to keep me from bringing the cup to my own lips. Seeing this, the other firefighter reached over and broke up the ice at the elbow bend of my coat, loosening it so I could maneuver my hot coffee. After he free'd up my two elbows, I did the same for him. As firefighters approached the coffee van, it started to look like a scene out of the Wizard of Oz where the Tin Man needed to have all his joints oiled before he could move.

Snow brings another set of problems, especially when a rapid response is imperative.

In 1979 we worked through one of the worst blizzards I'd ever experienced. I had only heard tales of the earlier 1967 blizzard, but some of the lessons learned then helped us out with this challenge that lasted 4 or 5 days.

Our problems with snow were enhanced due to having a large initial snowfall followed by several days of additional snow, dumping tons of snow on top of a previous layer of deep snow. The number one challege was getting our rigs or ambulances to where they were needed when called. Another problem was that most of the city's several hundred fire hydrants were impossible to locate; they were buried under several feet of plowed snow from the streets.

If we were successful negotiating a couple of engines and ladder truck through the deep snow to a house fire, we could pull all the hose we wanted, but until an engine hooked up to a hydrant, we only had what water we had onboard, a mere 500 gallons.

If we were lucky, the homeowner or neighbor would remember where the hydrant was located and we could quickly start digging. Otherwise, crews on the first few such responses had to use long metal rods to poke around through curbside snowdrifts, some taller than the firefighters themselves, until they hit something metallic. Then the frantic digging would start in hopes that the object would actually be a hydrant.

Our inability to quickly locate a hydrant in an emergency prompted the fire department to take drastic measures. They obtained several city water maps, and distributed copies of the appropriate city district to each engine company. These maps were not entirely accurate. They had a tolerance of a few yards, give or take, but could at least help determine what side of the street to search. Then all off duty firefighters were called in. Every department vehicle was dispatched city wide and firefighters armed with water maps, long metal rods and shovels of all types were sent out to dig out every hydrant in the city.

In crews of two or three, we'd make our way to our assigned area and begin looking for hydrants. Where the chart told us a hydrant existed, we stopped and began poking through the tall snow-plow generated curbside mountains of snow with the long metal rod until we hit something. Then the shovels would come out and we'd not only dig our way to the hydrant, but clear an area around the entire hydrant and a clear path to the street. Once done, we'd move on poking through drifts where the next hydrant was supposed to be.

We worked around the clock for nearly 48 hours, with teams of two or three working for four hours locating and digging, then taking a two hour break for rest or sleep.

Any calls for the ambulance also included an engine leading the way and forging what path it could for the Mobile Intensive Care Unit. Most times this worked, but during this storm, a couple of calls had problems, resulting in another station responding from another direction or even a neighboring community.

One call for a stranded motorist having a heart attack was called in by a receptionist in a nearby office building. The motorist was on our city's south side near the airport. All traffic on Touhy Avenue and Higgins Road was at a standstill due to the snow and looked more like a snowpacked parking lot than a major State highway. With the volume of stranded vehicles, no plows could get through, and as we were soon to find out, no ambulances could either.

An anticipated success quickly turned out to be a failure. Though the ambulance did finally manage to reach the motorist as he went into full arrest, the continuing snowfall and more stranded vehicles blocking the roadway prevented the ambulance from getting to any nearby hospital or trauma center. Even a helicopter was considered, but there was no nearby landing area available. The ambulance crew, along with the help of an engine company crew, could only perform CPR for so long before the attending physician on the radio finally called for them to stop.

It was several hours before the ambulance could eventually return to service back at the station. It's first stop once the snow was cleared was to drop off one of the storms' early casualties at the ER.

In between the severe cold and severe heat, we also had to deal with periodic floods and the ocassional tornado. Still, unlike some of our counterparts in other parts of the country, we didn't have to deal with hurricanes or earthquakes. As one local firefighter compared our natural disasters with those on the west coast, "I'd rather do the 'twist' than 'rock and roll' anytime." To each his own, I guess.

Chapter Twelve

The Field

The beginning of each winter in the Midwest is usually an eye-opener. Furnaces dormant for the summer months start fires, and icy roads catch drivers out of practice and still a bit too quick on the brakes. Accidents were heavy one particular night in early December, and both holiday preparations and emotions were in high gear.

The first real cold snap of the year magnifies the depression that some people feel around the holidays, especially those recently unemployed and the lonely folks that are particularly sensitive to the high spirits that surround them.

On this night, a 45 year old father of three, despondent over money problems and several bouts with surgery, quietly put on his coat and secretly slipped a .38 revolver that he'd retrieved from his bedroom drawer into his pocket. He told his wife and 13 year old son that he was going out for a walk. His wife, sensing his depression, asked if he'd wait so she could go with him. He said no, and went out the door.

The teenaged son, recognizing the worried expression on his mom's face, rushed to get his boots and coat so he could follow his father into the cold night air, the temperature still dropping a degree or two each hour. Once outside, his dad was already out of sight, but his fresh tracks in the snow guided his son down the block toward a large open field about four houses down. Just before reaching the field, the boy heard a loud pop that sounded like a large firecracker along with a flash of light that reflected on the leaves of a tree in the parkway across the street.

Running in the direction of the flash, he nearly tripped over the body lying in the snow near the middle of the field. As his eyes continued to adjust to the darkness, he recognized his father face down, on his right side, his legs crossed after twisting a bit as he fell. He heard a slight and muffled gurgling sound. Getting no response, the son ran to the closest house - one of several whose back yards bordered the field -- and banged on the door for help.

Fire Station #3 was only a few blocks away, so the ambulance arrived in less than three minutes after the surprised neighbor called for help. The son had panicked and ran back to his own house to get his mother. She was just arriving at the field as the ambulance pulled up, still buttoning her coat as she ran, hoping for the blessing of mistaken identity.

Paramedics, armed with flashlights in addition to their medical cases and other gear, followed the boy and his mother to the now silent clump in the snow. They bathed the body with two streams of light, partially reflected by the blood that glared up from the stark white background of snow. The mother dropped to her knees and began to cry as her son knelt beside her, alternately consoling her and erupting into sobbing spasms of his own.

As one paramedic checked for life signs, merely a perfunctory action at this point, the other corralled the mother and son away toward a neighbor's house as the police arrived. Within the next hour and a half, the police took photos, triangulated the position of the body, and made some quick diagrams while a few patrolmen held back a growing number of neighbors and spectators who had assembled nearby.

Traffic on the street slowed and came to a halt several times as gapers squinted through their frosted car windows. A motorist honked to get traffic moving, only to stop himself when he was in a better viewing position. Nearby yards filled with families leaning over or up against their shrubs and picket fences straining to see what had happened.

The police response to this apparent suicide was larger than usual because a gun was involved and had been discharged. One police officer had a scuffle with a local photographer who, ignoring orders to stay back, had crossed the hastily stretched police tape and had approached the body while quickly snapping a series of motor-driven exposures for his paper. A pair of detectives circled the body, shivering in their three-quarter length coats, making suggestions to the Evidence Technician before returning to their warm car. I overheard one comment to his partner that they had "made their appearance."

Once the Medical Examiner had examined the body where it lay, he left for the hospital or morgue - wherever the police were to transport the body after all the necessary photos had been taken. The paramedics assisted a rookie police officer who had been assigned to transport the body in what we used to refer to -- in pre-politically correct days -- as a paddy wagon. As the wagon left, the crowd quickly thinned and eventually disappeared. The biting cold had overcome curiosity, and the show was over.

I had responded with two others on Ladder Truck 83 to provide lighting for the scene as police did their scene investigation. When we moved to reclaim our flood lights and return them to the truck, I paused for a moment to look at the impression the body had left in the snow and the hundreds of footprints that encircled it.

In the center was a deep pool of coagulating blood growing darker against the surrounding snow. I knew that this field was used by elementary school kids as a short cut to a nearby school. Somehow, nobody thought about the kids who would be passing this spot in the morning. Using the side of my boots, I scraped at the snow around the blood, mounding the snow over the thickening and clotting remnants that contrasted so grimly with the white field.

Traffic returned to normal pace, and lights in the homes bordering the field began to go out as the occupants shifted their attention from the recent excitement outside their window back to warm beds or the late movie on TV. In the field, the smooth snow cover was marred in only one area, with spindly arteries of footprints radiating in several directions from a mound of snow. Even the footprints were beginning to fill in as the snow began falling again, almost as if on cue.

I walked back toward the ladder truck, then I heard a sound. Turning, I saw a rabbit racing across the snowy field. It stopped, waited a few brief seconds as the distance between us increased, then darted into a cluster of bushes.

The field was empty again.

Chapter Thirteen

Make a Hole, and Make It Wide

Firefighters train extensively on specialized operations that many would otherwise consider just plain fun. How many people wouldn't jump at the chance to smash windows, kick in doors, or -- the ultimate rush -- tear open a car with the "Jaws of Life"? Think of the pent-up frustration and tension that can be expended by taking out a large picture window with the swing of the ax, or the sheer joy of ripping off the entire roof of a car using specialized tools and cutters. As first-responding firefighters, we'd get to do a lot of that, but relieving stress was not the objective. Sometimes it is the only way to safely extract an individual from the twisted metal conglomeration of a smashed automobile. Or, having no key for buildings or other structures, we'd need to make forcible entry into an apartment, home or business to search for occupants or extinguish a fire.

Most of the equipment that firefighters train with involve prying, cutting, smashing, breaking, tearing or chopping.

As a result, it's not uncommon for some adrenalin-charged first responding firefighters to make forcible entry their first instinct. Since seconds count in both medical and fire emergencies, speed is essential and there's no time to search or wait for a key. If we find a door is locked and we need to get in immediately, we'll break in. It's what we do.

"Make a hole, and make it wide", has long been a standard phrase used by firefighters who aren't the most patient types when responding to a call. It helps paramedics and firefighters get through a crowd at an emergency scene, and the same philosophy is applied whenever making forcible entry. There's a reason that firefighters often refer to a fire ax as the "key to the city."

Knowing this, many business owners, either through experience or at the suggestion of their insurance company, will install a "firemen's key box" at a strategic or main entrance so that in the event of an automatic fire or system trouble alarm, responders can access the keys needed to make entry. Usually, after a property owner had paid for the replacement of an expensive door, glass entryway, or repair a hole smashed through the wall, we'd find a nice shiny new emergency key box in place near the door the next time we had to respond.

Locks aren't the only obstacles to making an entry. During any fire or following a traffic accident, structural damage alone can sometimes become a greater barrier than any lock ever made. Vehicles involved in high speed accidents can twist and compress into nearly unrecognizable masses. Sometimes it's visually difficult to distinguish the front from the back, or the top from the bottom when first arrving on the scene. A driver or passenger may not be where you'd expect to find them. A few times, we didn't even find a victim until after pulling the vehicle apart. Another time, a second victim was discovered wedged beneath the first victim, both of them jammed tightly under the dashboard on the passenger side.

In a structure fire or a building damaged by explosion, collapse, or weather disaster, gaining entry is only the first obstacle. Large structural components may need to be cut or moved, using specialized tools in addition to brute strength. Floors or walls may need to be opened where doors or stairwells no longer exist. Firefighters have had to use their axes, for example, to chop through a non-load bearing wall through to the next room after finding the doorway blocked by either fire or debris following a partial collapse.

When I joined the department in the early 70's there were few power tools firefighters could rely on at an emergency scene. In addition to a collection of pry bars, crow bars and other tools, we often depended on a tool invented decades before called a "Halligan Tool", designed in 1948 by a New York City firefighter. A curious looking cross between a crow bar, pry bar, pick ax and battering ram, it has become one of the most common manual forcible entry tools used by fire departments worldwide, and can be often spotted slipped into a firefighter's rescue belt. One end could be used as a crow bar, the pick to begin openings in a wall, and the prying end would help separate a door from the jam. Sometimes it became just a big hammer or battering ram. It's uses were limited only by the user's imagination and the situation encountered.

Some rescue operations needed more than just a few firefighters all lifting or pulling at once. In the early days, we used a manually operated pair of hydraulic spreaders called a Porta-Power. These were ussed to pry open a smashed car door or even lift up a section of a car. Directed by calls of "Up on red, down on blue, down on red, up on blue", two firefighters would alternately pump up on one set of hand operated hydraulic jaws while releasing the pressure on another. Wooden blocks would be jammed in as openings widened, and eventually a patient could be accessed or extracted. Another curious system involved a variety of heavy duty rubber bladders – their construction reminded me of flattened steel radial tires – that could be inflated from one of the breathing tanks carried on each engine. They came in various sizes, and when used in conjunction with wood cribbing or spacers, firefighters could literally lift an entire vehicle off the ground as the bladders expanded using just compressed air. It was tedious and took time, but it worked.

Eventually, these were replaced by generator powered hydraulic spreaders commonly known as the "Jaws of Life", which not only provided powerful spreading and lifting power, but could also be used quickly as cutters that rescuers could use to literally remove the top of an automobile in minutes, allowing for complete access to an injured victim.

In the mid 70's, and assigned to the ambulance at the time, we responded along with an engine and ladder truck to a reported vehicle rollover. The engine always responded to vehicle accidents to deal with any potential fuel spill or fire. The ladder truck was also dispatched anytime a vehicle accident involved a rollover or the report of a trapped individual since it carried all of our extrication and specialized rescue equipment. Since the accident was near our municipal border with neighboring Park Ridge, IL, they also dispatched an additional ambulance to the scene as part of a long-standing jurisdictional mutual aid agreement.

As we pulled up on the accident scene, there was one car overturned laying on its roof, but its only occupant, the driver, had already crawled out and was waiting for us to arrive. Another car, a four door sedan, was upright, smashed in on the drivers side, and positioned diagonally in the center of the four lane street. Police had already stopped all traffic in both directions and were keeping a growing crowd of mid-day spectators off the street and out of our way.

The driver of the second car was still behind the wheel. About 45 years old, heavy-set with a balding head, we could easily observer that he had a long, deep gash that started at the center of his forehead and ran up and along the top of his head. Headwounds bleed a lot because of the high volume of arteries and capillaries throughout the scalp. In addition to all the blood, the open wound exposed what looked like the bony texture of his skull. He was barely conscious with blood covering the right side of his face and still soaking his white shirt. He was slowly nodding and mumbling as if he was going in and out of a daze, so my partner reached in to help support his head. The driver's side doors were smashed in, so I moved to the passenger side. No matter how hard I pulled on the handles, neither door would open. I called for some pry bars because the ladder truck had not yet arrived. My partner had by now entered the vehicle through an open back window and was in the back seat area behind the victim using both hands to support the patient's head and neck while trying to further assess his condition. Another firefighter reached in and helped apply light pressure with a compress to the scalp wound that was still bleeding bright red arterial blood in small pulses whenever pressure was released.

I jammed the pry bar in between the passenger side door and the frame and attempted to pry the door away from the frame, jammed it in a littler further, pried some more and so on. Seeing I needed help, another firefighter joined me as we both leaned our weight into the bar. I heard the ladder truck pull up and yelled out that we needed the the Hurst Tool (Jaws of Life) right away.

As we pulled and pried, another crew was quickly setting up the Jaws, laying out the long hydraulic lines that connected the Jaws to a gas powered engine that provided considerable hydraulic pressure. Others attached specialized prying tips to the jaws to tear the doors off the vehicle. Soon after one firefighter gave a yank to the compressor's pull-start rope, we barely heard the voice of a teenage boy – aged around 12 or 13 – as he called out to us trying to be heard over the collective noise from the generator, nearby vehicles and firefighters also yelling back and forth.

"Did you try the door lock inside?"

The firefighter inside heard it too, and our eyes met for one embarrassing instant as I motioned for him to reach over and pull up the little plastic knob barely a foot away from him. With two fingers he pulled up the knob. A quick yank on the door handle and the door swung open wide.

Unfortunately, all the peripheral noise did not mask the stifled giggles nearby.

About a year later we responded to a report of smoke coming from a basement apartment. I was on the first engine of a full structure fire response consisting of two engines and a ladder truck. A barely discernible amount of smoke was coming from around the front door of the lower level apartment. A neighbor was there; he said he'd already pounded on the door several times and there was no answer. It was only about five or six steps down to the door, and I held off with my ax remembering the boy at the rollover accident a year before.

This time I carefully checked the door, jiggling it a couple of times and yanking it again. This door is definitely locked, I told myself, and with the Captain's high sign to proceed, I raised the fire ax to take out the whole door handle area.

Just as I raised my ax I heard a panicky and near falsetto scream.

"I have the key! I got the key right here!" yelled the frantic property owner who had just returned home.

We used the key and gained entry to find a frying pan of grease still sitting on a hot burner. The flames were easily extinguished with a lid, and the property owner was spared the additional expense of replacing his door. Had we waited a few more minutes the outcome could have been a lot worse.

At one fire scene following a quick knock-down – our term for a fast extinguishment of the fire – a local news photographer asked me, "How come you guys don't have a lot of big extra alarm fires?" He wondered why, when he'd respond to some surrounding communities who had larger fires, that most of our fires were smaller. I explained that by quickly getting into a building and putting out fires while they're still relatively small, they don't grow into extra-alarm blazes in the first place. Fast and aggressive interior attacks, as opposed to the "surround and drown" exterior attack depend on making entry quickly and opening up the structure to vent superheated air and toxic fumes.

A key, when available, is always preferrable to cutting, chopping, splitting or smashing. Though firefighters are often depicted as "smash first, ask questions later" zealots disregarding personal property, making forcible entry is often the difference between rescuing a potential victim now or just recovering a body later.

Chapter Fourteen

A Woman's Place is in the Home, and She Should Go There Right After Work

The firehouse was one of the last male dominated workplace environments. It seemed immune to the heightened women's rights movement in the 60's and 70's. There were few, if any, efforts to eliminate gender discrimination back then beyond replacing the term "fireman" with "firefighter". Some could argue that it was also one of the most entrenched communities of misogynistic holdouts, even more resistant than our public safety colleagues over at the police department.

Our reluctant transformation began in the late 1970's. Due to a shortage of municipal funds and a lack of new, qualified firefighters eligible for advanced paramedic training, our department was faced with the prospect of a 6 month period where we would not be able to adequately man our three Mobile Intensive Care Units (MICU). One unit was assigned to each of our three fire stations within the city and these units were the workhorses and center of our now active paramedic program. The current eligibility list had expired, and it could take six or more months to recruit, hire and train enough fully trained firefighter-paramedics and place them on shift.

Once our department had adopted the paramedic program, all new hires were required to not only complete training as a firefighter and EMT-A (Emergency Medical Technician -Ambulance) but additional in-depth training as an EMT-P (P for Paramedic) as a condition of continued employment. Reducing service levels would require the elimination of at least one of those MICU's, leaving a third of our community unprotected, or in the alternative, the entire city divided in half with only the two remaining MICU's providing emergency medical response. This could seriously affect the 4 to 6 minute emergency response time that had been the average within the community, and would increase the potential for deaths and additional property damage that can result from delayed responses.

From this politically charged public safety debate, a decision was made to temporarily hire civilian paramedics. These temps would live within the firehouse and provide only emergency medical services until the newest yet-to-be-hired firefighter recruits were hired and had completed their extensive paramedic training. Paramedic slots could be filled immediately and without the cost of the long term pension and benefit package then in place for career firefighter-paramedics.

The plan was a good one and would only last six to eight months. As soon as recruitment classified ads were drafted, however, it became apparent that since no firefighting would be involved, the hiring would include females. They would work the same 24 hours on 48 hours off schedule, sleep in the bunkroom, shower in the bathrooms and eat with us at the table. Short of a seismic anomaly or the impact of a large asteroid hitting our downtown area, this possibility of having women co-habit within the firehouse was a life-changing event for those of us working 24 hour shifts.

There was a predictable initial uproar among many seasoned firefighters. First, most felt that the firehouse was no place for females and that, if forced upon us, women should be housed separately. Some felt pressure from their wives who resented and were opposed to the close proximity of women with their husbands -- especially overnight in the bunkroom. Some administrators worried that having women around in a formerly closed environment would open up potential sexual abuse or harassment charges resulting from bad language, inappropriate speech or behavior. Nobody seemed to be looking forward to what was perceived as potential alien invasion.

Almost immediately, special educational sessions were scheduled to provide sensitivity training to all shift personnel – a new and unfamiliar topic in most firehouses. This was to help prepare the troops with both social and legal training and hopefully make the anticipated welcome of female civilians a smooth and productive experience for all concerned. Two sessions a day were planned, over a three day period, in order to train all three shifts and all three stations. The first session began with a bang.

Engine company 61 and 62 along with the crews from Truck 1 and two ambulances gathered in the basement training room. In retrospect, the first mistake in this plan was allowing time for the crews to banter and speculate among themselves as they waited nearly 10 minutes for the instructor to arrive. Once she entered the room, all defenses were already up, pre-conceptions were fully formulated and challenges were pre-loaded and waiting to be launched.

"Good Morning gentlemen, my name is Ms. Cooper," the young woman began as she moved to the head of the room and pulled an assortment of workbooks and printed matter from her brief case and spread them on the table next to her podium. She rattled off her psychology and social work references, never even making eye contact with her audience. Finally, after sorting her piles of literature and completing her introduction, she looked up and posed a question to the group.

"Before we begin, let's find out just where we all are on discussing the challenges that each of you will face welcoming a woman into your workplace," she said, walking to the front of the table. One hand went up in the back of the room.

"Yes? Please go ahead," she said. "Won't you stand up?"

A firefighter in the back of the room, fully primed during the extended wait before her arrival, stood up and proclaimed, "I believe that a woman's place is in the home, and that she should go there right after work." The room exploded in laughter.

Young Ms. Cooper had no retort for that, tried to ignore the comment and, once the laughing and snickering had subsided, solicited more input hoping for something more tolerable or workable to use as a launching point. Unfortunately, she had failed to establish any credibility or confidence from the group when she arrived, and the next 30 minutes became even worse for her. Eventually, addressing the room that was full of what she must have considered little more than blue-shirted cavemen, she admitted that she was unable to help us in any way, packed her materials and left the room.

Within the hour, the department Deputy Chief in charge of training and the Fire Chief had made it known to every firefighter that the next class, and every class that would follow, would be MUCH different. Everyone apparently believed it because each of us, facing the personal wrath of the Chief of the department, participated in sessions that were incident free and ultimately proved to be informative and productive for most attending.

As with most evolutionary changes, the actual experience was different from what most expected. Only two or three female paramedics were hired. One, at nearly six feet tall, was big enough to take on any male firefighter in the station. Another was a former private ambulance worker, but she lasted only a few weeks after discovering she was not able to deal with emergency situations. There was one, however, who made her mark in several ways.

When she walked into the firehouse kitchen closely trailing the Fire Chief and our shift Captain, every eye locked on her blond hair and how her blue uniform tapered to non-standard hourglass form. The badge on her shirt, along with her nametag "DONNA", almost faced the ceiling supported by what some would call a "perky" chest. Her uniform shirt and pants were joined by a shiny black leather belt on a petite waist. Standard issue uniform pants did little to disguise the form beneath as the crease at the bottom of each pants leg broke slightly in proper fashion at the top of her small, shiny black oxfords. This was not a shape we were used to seeing inside of a fire department work uniform.

The striking blond instantly epitomized what most wives were worried about. She entered the room walking in decisive and purposeful steps along with perfect posture -- enhancing her form that was so out of place in a room full of muscles, an occasional tattoo and a preponderance of mustaches.

"Gentlemen, I'd like you to meet Donna Wilson," said the Chief now having our undivided attention. "Donna is one of six civilian paramedics hired during our temporary shortage and will be assigned to this shift."

The Chief ran through our names and ranks in an official introductory tone and then added, making sure he made direct eye contact with each one of us to make sure we understood that we'd be answering to him personally for any problems, assured her that "...these guys will help you settle in and show you the ropes. Right guys?"

The Chief left the room. "OK, Randy and Jeff here are manning 71 (the MICU) today," said the Captain as he also headed for the door.

"You'll spend today and next shift riding along as third man to learn our SOP's before riding as shotgun," he added just before the door closed behind him.

Civilian paramedics, in addition to being restricted from any firefighting duties, were also not cleared to drive Fire Department emergency vehicles. Most ambulance crews are teams of two, with one often dubbed the "driver", while the paramedic riding in the back with the patient is called the "Doc". Usually teams take turns in both positions, but the new civilian paramedics lacked the emergency driving training and experience of sworn personnel, and were not allowed to drive.

The first week or two having Donna in our midst for 24 hours may have been a bit tense, but there was no outward hostility or overt challenges from anyone. Our speech patterns, which had cleaned up dramatically when she was first assigned, gradually returned to the normal excessive use of the "F" word and others as we quckly found Donna well versed in firehouse vocabulary herself.

Since she had no firefighting duties, our contact and interaction was only on medical responses and in-station. In the kitchen, lounge and bunk room, Donna was completely at ease. At night she slept in a t-shirt and leotards she donned after using the shower which – for an hour each evening – required a homemade cardboard placard with the words "Female Occupied" written in large black marker. A separate single bathroom in one of the front offices provided her privacy as well.

In the bunkroom, the leotards may have offered her full coverage, but since they were form fitting, many of the guys found themselves feigning sleep some mornings as they peered out from under a blanket to watch her make her bed. A couple of firefighters initially slept on couches in the dayroom, one after a strong and insistent suggestion from his wife.

Donna proved to be more than just efficient on ambulance calls. At the time, medical responses were classified as either BLS (Basic Life Saving) or ALS (Advanced Life Saving). Most BLS calls could be handled by the ambulance crew themselves, while traffic or industrial accidents or any ALS call also required an engine company. Depending on the call, there may be a need for tools and equipment, extinguishment or washdowns, or in the case of full blown cardiac arrest or other life threatening malady, several additional hands may be needed to assist with patient treatment and transportation.

Donna was an outstanding paramedic. Those of us who worked with her on shift came to realize that her diagnostic talents in the field were uncanny. Soon most followed her lead, although at first reluctantly, then almost as SOP when she was there. Within months, on calls ranging from severe auto accidents to full cardiac arrests, we found that she was nearly unshakable and clearly knew was she was doing.

Constantly finding ways to improve things within the MICU, she quickly re-arranged the materials stored throughout the rig, moving them to more accessible locations or situating them based on how often they were accessed. Compartments and drawers soon even sported color-coded labels. This innovation was soon emulated by the other two stations in the department.

Once, after watching one of the engineer-drivers on Engine 61 unfold a canvas roll containing open ended wrenches of various sizes, she went home and designed a similar cloth storage roll that provided pockets for the different sizes of esophageal and intubation airways and tubes used on the MICU. Then, instead of a paramedic rifling through a box of loose tubes and equipment to quickly access the desired tube or tool during an emergency as a patient struggled for air, a paramedic could pull a velcro tab and unroll all the available sizes, instantly visible for rapid access. It was so well received that she was asked to make three more for the other two stations and the reserve MICU.

At the time I took photos of the roll and, with her permission, sent it in with an article to FIREHOUSE Magazine. I even included a diagram along with the list Donna had given me of materials needed to make one. Within a year after the article was published the design was utilized by a major national supplier of emergency medical equipment and is a standard item offered in EMS catalogs to this day.

Donna made her mark in many ways. Instead of challenging the old boys' club, she took them head on, never complaining but setting examples instead.

The civilian paramedics also provided support services on the fireground. Once, at a fire response in the wee hours of the morning, I was coming out of the structure's front door with another firefighter after helping knock down a nasty basement fire. I was pulling off my helmet and opening my coat as we came down the sidewalk to drop our air packs off at the engine. Standing by with the MICU, Donna met us at the engine and -- as she did with all firefighters coming out for break or new air tank – she checked us out to see if we needed any help or were hurt in any way.

"How you doin'?" she asked as she handed each of us a large plastic cup of cold hydrant water from an open engine port. "Anything burned, broken or bumped?" We gladly accepted the water, noting that we were okay.

As I passed by, Donna reached up and pulled back my firecoat collar a bit, revealing dark, red streaks -- a bit of minor par-broiling I took as a blast of water spray was instantly turned to hot steam around my unprotected neck. It was a common occurrence prior to the issue of fire resistive Nomex hoods a year or so later.

"Bit of a steam burn here." she said, handing me a couple of ice cubes. "Rub that neck down for a bit until these melt," she said.

I complied, and feeling the burning ease immediately, I said, "Thanks, Mom."

After seven months Donna and the five other civilian paramedics were advised that their time was up and that newly trained firefighter paramedics would be taking their place. Some of them went on to apply to different fire departments while others moved over to private ambulance jobs. Donna continued in school, helping train new paramedics, and eventually earned her Ph.D. in Immunology.

Her six months were especially challenging for our fire department. We were faced with not only a major construction accident and an historic blizzard, but the largest civilian air disaster in US history when American Airlines Flight 191 crashed shortly after takeoff into our southern border. Her short time helping break the gender barrier in the firehouse helped pave the way for the women who would soon follow and eventually make firefighting a co-ed occupation.

Within a few years our department redesigned the agility test with the intention of more accurately reflecting specific job-related activities and allowing more women a better chance to compete. Soon after, our department hired its first female firefighter. She served over 20 years, many of those years as a Fire Inspector. She also earned a Master's degree in Engineering that served her well following retirement.

To date, no other female has been hired.

Chapter Fifteen

Space Center Firefighting & Rescue

I've always been a space nut. As a lifelong science fiction fan, I'm always fascinated whenever current science fact emulates something I'd read in a fiction or fantasy book years before. Like other baby boomers, I was continually exposed to the rapid series of space related accomplishments that followed the first Sputnik scare in the 50's. It seemed like every year a new launch or a discovery by astronomers would grab a headline and further reduce the line between science fact and fiction.

As NASA scientists developed bio-sensors and radio telemetry so they could monitor the life signs and health of astronauts in orbit or on the moon, they were also providing the foundation of the modern paramedic program. Engineers who worked on materials that would stand up to extreme heat and friction during re-entry or as part of rocket propulsion systems didn't know at the time their labors would lead to heat resistance cookware and the fire resistive fabrics used by race car drivers and firefighters. The fire service, along with major industries, were the recipients of many space race technology spinoffs that continue to save lives every day.

The idea for a fire service space story came in the summer of 1985, when I had a chance to visit the Kennedy Space Center (KSC) as part of a Florida vacation. I was riding on one of the center's tour buses as it drove from the visitor center toward one of the two shuttle launch pads. At the one-mile marker or the A-5 point – the distance between the sign and the actual launch pad – the bus passed a small armored vehicle. The driver explained over the loudspeaker how a handful of firefighters stood by this vehicle during the actual launch in case of an emergency that would require them to respond to the pad and perform a rescue. "These firefighters are the closest human beings to the pad during the launch, other than the astronauts themselves," he said.

That's when the plan popped into my head. "You know, I gotta come back here and do a story on this," I quietly muttered into my wife's ear. My tone was certainly less-than-humble. Pointing to the armored rover as we passed, "And I want to get a ride in that vehicle." After returning home days later, I sent my proposal to FIREHOUSE Magazine with a request for an assignment letter so I could begin the process of gaining the necessary press credentials.

Within a few weeks, I received my assignment letter and was able to schedule some time with the KSC Fire Chief, to coordinate some vacation time from the department so that it would coincide with an actual scheduled shuttle launch. My intent was to document the activities of the Kennedy Space Center fire department before, during and after a space shuttle launch.

The two-day drive to Florida's east coast allowed my

excitement and anticipation ferment and grow long before I arrived at the forward gate leading into the Space Center. There, I would check in and obtain my press credentials, parking placard, detailed listings of restrictions, site maps, and a hefty press kit for the upcoming launch. Once checked in, with my press pass hanging around my neck, I drove into the center. I followed a map, that I had penciled in a large "X" marking the location of the Space Center fire station, to meet the Space Center Fire Chief, Richard Cross.

As I made my final turn, I was excited to see that the station was located directly across the street from the massive Vehicle Assembly Building. The KSC folks referred to this to as the world's largest building. Chief Cross met me when I arrived, and once my vehicle was parked and secured behind the station, whisked me off in his car to a NASA headquarters office building. Once in his office, we had a "meeting of the minds" discussion where I felt that the Chief was sizing me up and determining if I was a friendly or adversarial type. Once I had assured him that I wasn't a professional journalist, but in fact a working firefighter who had taken vacation days to chronicle a visit, he relaxed and let his guard down. Had it been otherwise, I thought later, my access and welcome may not have been so warm and informative. I was soon to learn that Cross was a retired Battalion Chief with the Washington, D.C. Fire Department, so his concerns over my motives may have been more knee-jerk than outright cynical.

Together we had lunch with one of KSC's public relations representatives who not only provided additional packets of information and stacks of photos but a prepared itinerary for the next three days. The last day would be the scheduled shuttle launch at noon. Learning that I was a working firefighter and regular contributor to a major fire service magazine, some additional flexibility was given to the Chief in the access that

I would enjoy. It was another illustration of how firefighters feel connected and maintain a bond no matter where they are from. I was happy to take full advantage of the privilege and not abuse it.

Another door opener for me, I believe, was that one day of the itinerary also included an Air Force Staff Sergeant from Vandenburg Air Force Base. The California base also served as a launch area for many NASA and military space missions and was a potential back up location for the Kennedy Space Center's future shuttle launches or support activities. The sergeant had some unspecified Vandenburg launch area responsibilities and was using this visit to become familiar with KSC operations. I was happy to keep my ears wide open in the wake of his inquiries as well.

The first day was spent talking with the Chief and collecting facts and figures, and taking a tour of two KSC fire stations. All fire and rescue services provided by the department were through EG&G Florida, a private contractor that provided nearly all support services for the sprawling complex. That included, in addition to fire and rescue, a wide menu of services ranging from fuel delivery and distribution systems to trash collection on the site.

The space center's fire department provided services for a complex literally the size of a small town; the KSC worker population grew from 14,000 to 16,000 before, during and immediately following a scheduled launch. Then on launch days, with the arrival of 40,000 observers and media, 7,000 or more automobiles and busloads of VIP's, the KSC FD responsibilities rivaled that of a large US city. Unique to the center was a vast network of fuels, propellants, and other volatile chemicals and cryogenics needed for launch, orbital maneuvering, cooling and more.

On my second day I had a chance to ride around a bit in the little M-115 armored personnel carrier that had ignited my initial interest when my tour bus drove by it almost a year before. At a location designated as the "A-5" point, less than a mile from the launch pad, a group of firefighters would stand by this armored transport vehicle prior to each launch in case they were needed to quickly go in and get astronauts out of the shuttle, perhaps due to leaking chemical fumes, technical malfunction, or fire on the launch pad. They would ride up the elevator to the 190 foot level and open the shuttle entry way with special tools stored nearby. Rescuers could not wear standard air packs and still get in and out of the small round entry. In case of toxic fumes or smoke, rescuers wore several smaller low volume pressurized air tanks on their backs, and strapped others to their legs. Some were for rescuers to breathe from, and others were for giving to the one or more astronauts inside.

If the shuttle occupants were not conscious, rescue personnel would attach a special metal slide apparatus from inside the shuttle cabin, and slide the astronauts out one by one. Once out of the orbiter, they'd be placed into one of two emergency slide wire cages and sent streaming down a nearly quarter-mile zip line to relative safety. Astronauts routinely trained on these escape methods as well, along with the firefighters.

That second day was an especially long one spent visiting various areas key to launch support services. I learned about training operations and preparations conducted by the OSCO (Off Shore Contingent Operations) Team, about the shuttle landing strip, weather control, and the shuttle launch pad itself.

The OSCO teams were made up of several firefighter-paramedics who routinely trained in case of a shuttle launch abort. They would be airlifted by helicopter to wherever the shuttle might come down within several miles of the launch pad – whether on land or along the Atlantic coastline. A duplicate OSCO team, I learned, was dispatched days before with all the same equipment to Dakar, West Africa to perform similar rescue operations should the shuttle reach further downrange.

Each team was equipped with rescue equipment, lines, cutting devices, medical supplies, tools, and many other items. All of these were carefully packed and secured inside a rescue raft strapped to the bottom of a helicopter. Should the need arise, the crew would immediately be airlifted and dropped in the ocean or quickly deposited on land near the downed shuttle.

Prior to each launch, the OSCO teams and other KSC firefighters brushed up on procedures using a mockup shuttle cockpit located near the press site complex. The actual-sized wooden mock-up can either be laid on its belly, to simulate a ground landing, or tipped vertically, to resemble its posture on the launch pad itself. Or the entire structure can be placed in a nearby pond, so crews can practice water rescues with all the necessary equipment.

The fire captain describing these procedures to us that afternoon spoke with an extremely thick southern Florida accent. Apparently I failed to take this into account when I thought I heard him explain. "…and this crane is utilized to help place the shuttle crew compartment mockup into the pond for training porpoises."

"Training porpoises?" I blurted out with a bit of incredulity, imagining Flipper or other highly trained dolphins working alongside human rescue divers carrying lifelines around the downed spacecraft.

"Purrrrposes, dammit. I said training purposes," he gruffly responded, cleaning up his pronunciation a bit for my mid-western ears.

I weighed my questions a bit for the rest of the afternoon.

Throughout the rest of the day, I saw where crews trained on techniques used to fight fuel fires like none ever fought in Des Plaines, Illinois. At one site, hypergolic fuels – chemicals that only need to come in contact with each other to ignite – are introduced into a small center pit from different directions. Once they meet, they ignite – more like mini-explosions – creating a sound like claps of thunder just a few feet away. These fuels, in a more controlled environment, are used in maneuvering the orbiter in zero gravity.

We visited the shuttle landing strip, driving out to the spot where years of shuttle orbiters had landed precisely, creating a blackened area barely 30 feet in diameter. Pointing to what looked like a floating log or piece of wood in the nearby adjacent canal, the Chief introduced me to George, a large alligator that lived in the canal, and who, I was told, had been a resident there for more than 20 years.

"Oh, you can get closer for a picture if you want to," advised the Chief when I reached for my camera and stepped toward the canal.

"But I wouldn't advise it. George can outrun you easily in the short run if he wants to."

I stood my ground after hearing that, but continued to marvel at the fascinating contrast between the prehistoric reptilian throwback just a few yards away and the sprawling, futuristic complex that surrounded him in every direction.

That night provided an extra special treat. Having official press credentials, I was able to sign on for the special "RSS Rollback" photo op that evening. At midnight, precisely 12 hours before the scheduled launch the following day, the Rotating Service Structure that surrounds much of the launch vehicle as it stands on the pad is rolled back and away from the orbiter. At that time, several huge searchlights at the base of the pad bathe the white shuttle and huge rust colored main fuel tank in bright light for the rest of the night as preparations for launch continue. That night we were bused out to the launch pad for a chance to take some dramatic close-up photos. There, in the same driveway traveled by the huge transport system that carries the orbiter from the Vehicle Assembly Building to the launch pad, I had a chance to stand in the still damp sand and gravel and click away with my camera.

The next morning, I checked out of my hotel and drove in to KSC early before the scheduled noon launch of STS (Space Transport System) 61-A, which would carry the first German Space Lab (D-1) into orbit as part of the International Space Station. I gleaned a few tips from more seasoned press photographers while on the bus the night before, and I made sure I was on site in front of the press viewing area by 7 am even though the launch was set for 12 Noon. Once there, I placed my camera tripod at the edge of the ground near the leading edge of a canal. A giant digital clock, one that I recognized from watching countless launches on TV, was several yards behind me, and the VIP viewing stand further still. This spot was the closest spot available for photographers to record the launch.

In anticipation of this once in a lifetime opportunity, I borrowed a long-range zoom lens along with a motor drive for my Nikon camera. After consulting with other photographers, I set the proper aperture and exposure and was ready to begin a rapid series of exposures once the launch began. Now, still before 8 a.m., I draped my jacket over the empty tripod to hold my spot and went off to find breakfast and to make some additional notes before the launch. The cafeteria used by KSC workers and visitors was just a block away from the massive Vehicle Assembly Building and the launch viewing area, and was appropriately named "The Lunch Pad".

Both the crowd and my excitement grew as noon approached. This wasn't a particularly special launch as some are, and had nowhere near the press coverage that some of the earlier launches enjoyed. I had no way of knowing at the time, of course, that the shuttle waiting on the pad for a noon launch would be flying its last successful mission. This orbiter, named "Challenger", would explode several months later just 73 seconds after lifting off the pad.

Both luck and ideal weather were on my side that day, as there were no unscheduled delays in the countdown, and the huge orbiter lifted off on time. I started taking photos when the first gush of white steam, created by the huge volumes of water unleashed below the shuttle's engines to help suppress both sound and vibration, began to puff up and billow around the shuttle. When the sound hit me, it felt like I was hit with a large pillow or cushion. I felt a large pounding against my chest, along with a roar so loud that it changed quickly to a crackling sound slapping away at my ears. At the same time, I felt the ground begin to vibrate and shake beneath my feet. This was no ordinary sound. This sound was so big I could almost taste it. Nothing I've heard since would compare. I kept my finger pressed down on the shutter release as the camera's motor drive continued to take multiple exposures. As the camera snapped and cycled, I kept sinking almost to my knees tilting the camera upward while keeping my eye to the viewfinder, following the gleaming vehicle's trailing fireball as it rose overhead.

After the launch, a few photographers were high-fiving each other as the sound diminished and the huge column of smoke rose miles into the sky and up through the clouds. Feeling like a pro for the moment, I even slapped a few palms myself. We all eventually gathered up our tripods, packed away the cameras and headed for the parking lot nearby.

I had gathered up all of my article notes before the launch, the car was already packed and I had no more interviews or visits scheduled. The launch was my last photo op, so I headed back home to Illinois to finish the article and send it in.

That was in October of 1985, and it wasn't until March of 1986 that the article was published in FIREHOUSE Magazine, almost two months after the tragic explosion of the Challenger orbiter whose last safe launch I'd witnessed several months before.

See Addendum Two, "Training for Shuttle Blast Off".

Chapter Sixteen

A Jelly Donut
Will Have to Do

The Klaxon horn blasted shortly after 3 a.m., followed by a report of a nearby rear-end vehicle crash with one overturned auto fully involved in flames. Pulling out of the station onto Oakton Street, we could see the glow and flame-illuminated smoke rising from the center of the street several blocks to the west. PD (the police department) was already responding and one squad screamed past the station as our bay doors were opening.

Any reported traffic accident with injuries required at least an ambulance and an engine, with the first-in unit determining the need for any additional MICU or rescue truck. With two cars involved and flames reported, they were already on the way.

Car fires are a tricky business. While some may consider them a minor fire compared to a structure fire, firefighters learn that a burning vehicle is potentially a lethal collection of hazards and unpredictable explosions. Depending on the make and year of a vehicle, the car may contain a series of sealed piston-like devices that are integral parts of its bumper system or merely serve to dampen the closing of the front hood. Heated enough by impinging flames, these devices can turn the bumper into a knee-shattering projectile shooting out and away from the front or rear of a vehicle. Hood pistons can blow and turn long piston rods into metal shafts propelled as if from a crossbow or spear gun. Burning magnesium parts can flash with flames actually fed by the oxygen from the water applied. Gas tanks that are part of a sealed fuel system can blow, but instead of the large orange mushroom cloud as depicted on TV action shows, these can ignite and spread a rapidly growing lake of burning gasoline around the vehicle engulfing anyone nearby.

Pulling up we saw an SUV completely overturned and fully involved in flames. A separate car, a more compact sedan, was directly behind it, slightly angled away from the SUV, with most of the front end smashed in and crunched considerably lower near the front bumper. We could see that the car had rear-ended the SUV with enough impact to literally flip the SUV over, at the same time rupturing the fuel tank and igniting it with a spark either from the car's battery or from metal impacting metal. One victim, a middle-aged female who was not wearing a seatbelt, was ejected from the SUV as it flipped. The driver of the sedan, obviously drunk, had already exited his car. He had some facial lacerations, but was barely aware of them.

Two of us were riding backwards that day, and we jumped off the rig and grabbed the on-board booster line to start knocking down the flames now fully encapsulating the SUV. Since most all of the windows were gone already, it was not difficult to quickly douse the flames which transformed the water, due to the now superheated metal, instantly into thick clouds of hot steam rising from the vehicle. The steam was so thick we had to search with our hands initially to determine if anyone was still inside. The vehicle was laying on it's roof, and the vehicle's upholstery, or what was left of the frames and springs, was now laying on the interior of the roof with other contents. The upended orientation of the vehicle added to the confusion until the steam started to diminish slowly from the top down. Hot metal continued to generate enough steam to block our view.

Leaning deep inside the car, I rested one arm on a solid surface below me, and strained to see what I could, squinting and trying to focus on something – anything – that looked familiar. Soot and blackened char was on everything, so it was hard to even discern specific shapes. As the steam slowly diffused, I spotted a small white patch, around an inch or so in diameter that stood out through the smoke and steam from the surrounding blackened landscapes. Squinting a bit more, the barely visible outlines around the patch were slowly coming into view. My eyes were still stinging from both sweat and dirty water when I recognized the white patch as part of a torso laying below me. A draft of air swept in and revealed a larger area for a second or two. That's when everything fell into place and I suddenly realized the white patch was a portion of a human skull where flesh had been burned away as if by a blowtorch. I was leaning just inches over the head of a charred body with the rest of the body curled slightly and the feet facing away from me.

We learned from the passenger that the victim was driving the SUV; she was several months pregnant and had been restrained by her seatbelt. She burned to death because her vehicle had been struck by a 24 year old drunk who had just left a bar in a nearby community in search of another bar that was still open.

The ambulance crew was gathering information from the inebriated and uncooperative drunk and learned that the bar he was coming from was a gay bar in the neighboring community. As with most first responders in the early to mid 1980's we were still learning about the spread of the relatively new condition known as AIDS, and we had all recently gone through several training sessions dealing with the hazards of blood-borne pathogens. At this early stage of our knowledge of this new hazard, any first responder with a suspected contact could expect to be subjected to extensive blood testing and, pending those test results, and having restricted contact with family members and others for several days until given the green light.

Emergency medical personnel nationwide were entering a period of both substantiated and imagined biological paranoia and were using new and enhanced protective measures with injured patients. The concern over blood-born pathogens gave us new protective masks and devices that allowed for safer emergency respirations than the old tried and true mouth-to-mouth technique.

In those days AIDS was still a new and mostly unknown, yet potentially devastating, hazard to first responders and we still had much to learn. Those new fears of ours, coupled with just plain anger combined as the drunken kid wailed and complained, asking for help, not even knowing he had killed the pregnant driver. Knowing full well that his injuries were at least not arterial, paramedics pulled the stretcher out the rig, slid it over to where the uncooperative kid sat on the curb and said, "Shut the &#@% up and get on the stretcher!" At least on that one night, the usual compassion for an injured stranger took a back seat to many new fears, and – at least for the moment – unfiltered bigotry.

We still needed to extract the body from the SUV, so that PD could transport the body to the morgue. We knew we couldn't just grab a severely burned corpse by the arms or legs and pull it out of the car. If we tried, flesh would literally separate from the bones in some areas and slide off in our hands. We needed to try and slip something under her and pull her out.

"Let's try to get a backboard under her," said the Lieutenant. "We can slide it under like a pizza oven." The metaphor – intended to describe the action and not as a joke – was an accurate one.

The backboard would only slide a few inches under the body, so we quickly gave that up. I suggested that we use the two coal shovels we had on the engine to pry the body up a bit so that the board would slide further. That worked, and we were able to slide the body off of the board onto the PD wagon's stretcher. Following a quick wash down of the accident scene after the police took all of their photos and measurements, and a tow truck had removed the sedan, we were released from the scene.

It was now approaching 6 a.m. The accident coincidentally happened less than 50 yards from a Dunkin' Donut shop. "Hey Lieutenant," I called out to as we moved toward the engine, "let's grab some donuts for back at the station." Being the cleaner of the three of us, the lieutenant agreed to go in and pick up a dozen.

Back at the station, it was approaching time for shift change, and the events of the past few hours were still sinking in. We traded the predictable comments regarding our disdain for the drunk driver, and the gallows humor kicked in right away, as it does with these calls, especially with the gruesome surprise that we found this time.

That particular shift had been especially grueling, having started 22 hours earlier with an apartment fire on the north side of town. That fire claimed a fatality as well. Our first-in crew discovered the burned remains of the senior citizen occupant who had failed to make it out of the apartment. Dealing with two fire fatalities in two separate fires within one shift was not common for us.

We sat around the large circular table in the kitchen. It was actually a large, old cable spool that firefighters many years before had finished off with wood and veneers. It had become the main table for all our meals. Jensen, our Engineer-Driver on the call, circled the table repeating a single phrase.

"I need some counseling. I need some counseling," he moaned sarcastically, holding the back of his hand dramatically to his forehead.

We had all recently discussed and laughed about an article concerning how some west coast city fire departments had hired post-event stress counselors following a local airline crash. We hadn't been exposed to that kind of progressive thinking as yet and, still entrenched in our unchecked macho attitudes, found the whole concept a bit laughable.

He continued slowly repeating with a feigned agony, "I need some counseling," and then stopped, turned toward the table and quietly reached out across the table.

"But a jelly donut will just have to do."

Chapter Seventeen

The Politics of Fire

In the 70's and 80's, many people didn't think that firefighting and labor unions had that much in common. At least for the young idealistic recruit, firefighting was considered to be a service often requiring the kinds of personal sacrifices that involved family, individual health and, in many cases, a crippling injury or even death. Unions, on the other hand, were known for reducing work hours and insuring proper health care. Some labor contracts even included workplace safety protection items. While all those are good things, some seemed contradictory to firefighting. For example, one day I was looking around department headquarters offices for a common swing-arm paper cutter – the type where you cut several sheets of paper at once with a downward stroke of a long handled blade. I was told by the Chief's secretary that those were not allowed since they were too dangerous. It was an "insurance thing," she said. Dangerous? Do they know what we all do for a living around here? I wondered.

I see unions through two separate lenses; one old and one much newer. The old traditional unions fought hard for almost all of the present day employee benefit packages and protections that most of us experience today, at least if we're actively employed. Child labor restrictions, workmen's compensation in case of an on-the-job injury, overtime and many workplace safety guarantees were the result of some dedicated, serious and oftentimes violent action on the part of unions. Many brave individuals were willing to go up against corporate battlements armed only with picket signs, sometimes facing a truckload of goons wielding baseball bats. As the years passed, those rights and protections became established and protected by law, so unions turned to other employee benefits such as paid vacations, holidays, health insurance and non-discrimination issues.

Some feel that modern unions have morphed into a large, corporate-like and self serving behemoth, draining paychecks even more through forced union dues, while union reps and managers enjoy six digit salaries and lucrative perks. Expensive lawyers, job actions or strikes – once only the nuclear option for the old unions fighting for basic rights – are now used to fight against employee contributions to health insurance or contributions into their own pensions.

The history of firefighter labor issues falls somewhere in the middle, taking a little of the good along with a little of the bad along the way. Full-time, paid firefighters were late to pick up the labor flag, but were forced to do so to prevent blatant political patronage in hiring, discipline and overall funding and operations. Where there weren't adequate Police and Fire Commission or Civil Service protections, or where those laws fell short, a collective bargaining agreement with a city or municipality offered the only protection during the lifetime of the contract. That agreement ensured that certain procedures would be followed, salaries and benefits would remain intact, and even serious issues such as equipment manning, and the effectiveness of many firefighting tools including turnout clothing and the like would be protected and would remain free from ever-changing political whims and, in some cases, just plain ignorance.

In the 1970's fire departments in the U.S. were still in the midst of a significant evolutionary shift, much like the periodic growth spurts that kids go through. Sometimes that evolution was rapid and smooth, and other times erratic and adversarial. Resistance to change was widespread. I remember seeing this sign displayed in a Chicago firehouse, "Chicago Fire Department: 150 Years of Tradition Unaffected by Progress". This expressed a sentiment common to many firehouses.

The 70's and 80's were decades of change, growth and of evolution, and the tailboard riding firefighter, wearing his canvas coat, rubber gloves and pull up boots – not to mention the old leather helmet with the soot-covered flip-down plastic eye protection – were becoming a thing of the past. The sight of arriving firefighters searching the engine cabinets for an airpack, was slowly disappearing as each seat on the engine was soon backed by a quick-mount airpack for each man. Even more dramatic was the shift from engine companies responding with firefighters with only advanced first aid training, an oxygen tank and relying on a funeral home ambulance for transport, to teams of trained paramedics manning modern and fully equipped Mobile Intensive Care Unit.

Firefighter Merit Pay: A three-year battle

For most cities with paid departments, it was a familiar cycle. Every 4 or 5 years or so, as new city aldermen were elected or a new mayor was sworn in, someone would have the same epiphany of a new way to save taxpayer dollars, usually at the expense of the fire department. Not understanding the economic distribution of manpower and scheduling provided by the 24 on, 48 off schedule using three shifts, we could almost predict when someone would suggest that "...things would be more cost-effective if those beds were taken out of the firehouse, and the men were placed on eight hour shifts". That way the day shifts could do the fire inspections, it was postulated, the evening shift could do the maintenance and the midnight shift could take on some paperwork duties for the city, or even fix parking meters, as often suggested.

Each time, the Chief would have to explain that doing so would require the hiring of an entire additional shift to account for off time, vacations, holidays and to keep overtime down. Our city would have to hire at least 15 or 16 additional employees, each with a full employment benefit package, too.

One year a new scheme took root, however, and thus began our department's longest and most emotionally charged labor battle. It eventually helped change the face of our department forever. Instead of across-the-board negotiated salary increases or cost of living adjustments, some new alderman suggested – supported by a study done by a recently hired consulting firm – that any annual increase should be granted based soley on merit, individually assessed by management. In our case, annual evaluations would be submitted by our company and shift officers. Increases would be awarded dependent on a firefighter's eventual evaluation score, placing him into one of 5 categories, the first being no increase, and the last being the largest increase. The city council believed that by doing so they could save money in the long run, the theory was, by denying increases to poor performers, and rewarding top performers.

Like many ideas that are great on paper and in theory, we soon learned it was difficult to objectively apply. The arguments over the concept of "pay for performance" were lengthy and bitter, especially from the firefighters who traditionally work together and live together as a team, where the final outcome of an emergency response was the result of that team effort. Proposed evaluation procedures could never be agreed upon, mainly since each manager required to rate an individual still did so drawing on a variety of individual biases and unique perspectives.

One example of the subjective application of evaluations was the difficulty of rating a new probationary firefighter after 6 month's of duty using a pre-defined numeric matrix that was still colored by individual value systems.

"Hey, with only 6 months on the job, how much could this rookie possibly know?" one officer might reason.

Another Captain, however, might believe "Hey, with only 6 months on the job, this firefighter knows quite a lot!" Same firefighter, same demonstrated skill level, but totally different evaluations.

The system as designed was flawed and allowed for too much of the potential favoritism and patronage that collective bargaining agreements and the Civil Service and Fire and Police Commissions were created to prevent.

In the mid 1980's municipal funds were drying up and budgets were being slashed. Political types everywhere were looking for ways to cut costs and were easily swayed by seemingly experienced and knowledgeable consultants. In our case, a merit based concept that may have been effective in a more measurable environment such as an industrial or manufacturing operation, was difficult to apply to a labor force that was much more unique in structure and function than those the consultants were familiar with.

Over two and a half years of collective bargaining battles on this issue led eventually to the end of our existing contract. We began the final six months of the battle not only without a contract, but extending the battle into local aldermanic and mayoral elections under the growing nearby specter of an unprecedented firefighters' strike in bordering Chicago.

Our local and autonomous collective bargaining group had resisted the temptation of affiliating with any of the larger unions such as the International Association of Firefighters not because we were anti-union, but because we had not been impressed at the time by professional labor representation. We had been able to deal with challenges on our own. We still paid our association dues, however, in order to deal with challenges or threats that would arise. During the protracted Merit Pay battle we used any tactic we could think of to send a message to the City Council that we were solidly opposed to the new salary evaluation system and that it was a flawed and dangerous concept. At one point the midwest head of the Teamsters Union agreed to come and speak to our group, knowing full well that it was a PR stunt and that we had no intention of joining their union.

Eventually a compromise was reached offering the city a longer time span in which to progress new hires from base pay to full pay at the Firefighter level and we avoided having our individual regular evaluations tied to salary increases. Instead of relying on salaries to control employees, evaluation procedures were updated allowing for better monitored progression and the creation of a paper trail necessary to help support disciplinary action or the termination of an employee.

Working together, both the firefighters' group and department management successfully crafted a fair and reasonable contract incorporating an internal grievance process, and we settled into a long period of relative peace between the forces, much of which survives today. The main lesson learned by both sides was to talk to each other directly rather than involve outside consultants – most or all of whom had never stepped into a fire station.

Perhaps it wasn't a panacea for all departments, but for years, instead of bitter job actions, contract battles and internal strife, our firefighters' association leadership team met periodically throughout the year with the Chief and administrative officers over breakfast at a local family restaurant.

Not all departments dealt with their differences in the same way, but for the time being at least, consultants, attorneys and memorandums of understanding, were soon replaced by bacon and eggs, juice and coffee.

Chapter Eighteen

Firefighters On Strike: An Outsiders' Inside Look

The Chicago firefighters' union in 1980 was having a lot of difficulty in gaining a new contract with the City of Chicago, as were other departments across the nation. At the same time that the Chicago firefighters were threatening to strike to regain civil service protections withdrawn a few years earlier by then Mayor Richard Daley and because of other manning and representation issues, my department was also in the midst of upheaval caused by protracted and adversarial contract negotiations.

Our local firefighters' association wasn't part of the International Association of Firefighters (IAFF) at the time; we were still part of a negotiated collective bargaining agreement forged by our own group and the city. Our dues were kept local; we paid our own attorney fees. As our Chicago colleagues fought it out with their city fathers, we were engaging in some tactics of our own in Des Plaines, including political involvement and lobbying, some minor work slowdowns and even an evening of informational picketing at city hall. A full blown strike, however, was never considered or even discussed as part of our own local labor battles.

The Chicago Firefighters' Union Local No. 2, the second largest firefighters' union in the country, by contrast, was threatening a strike vote continually, and as both sides dug in for the long haul, an IAFF meeting finally yielded a strike authorization vote by the rank and file, meaning that union leaders were authorized to call a strike if needed. The threat was made, and it was now rapidly approaching the time when a "put up or shut up" decision had to be made.

The City of Des Plaines, like many Chicago suburbs, borders portions of the City of Chicago, so it was natural that we'd be a target for the IAFF as they made preparations for their strike vote. Should a strike actually be called, even for just three shift days as was the plan to make a point, the threat would be more serious if the city understood that just calling on neighboring suburbs to cover wasn't an option. To this end, the IAFF called us all together one day for a pep talk.

I was part of our local negotiating team at the time, one of a triad of local association leadership along with two fellow firefighters – one who would one day become Chief of the department, and the other a City Alderman. Our association was in the midst of an ever increasing hostility between the firefighters, paramedics and engineers commonly referred to as "blueshirts" who were currently covered by collective bargaining and the opposing side: department officers and chiefs. We were locked in a bitter dispute on salaries and the performance ratings used to determine those salaries, and to the IAFF we looked like fertile ground as potential supporters.

In January of 1980, representatives from surrounding suburban firefighter unions and associations were invited to meet with union leaders of Chicago Firefighters Local #2. The Union President, along with his executive board, a union attorney, a strike chairman and a visiting IAFF representative sporting boots and cowboy hat were present to advise and question those who attended.

The discussion began with the possibility of a strike and the effect that the strike would have on individual suburban forces in the future. The IAFF rep explained that "Chicago would be the touchstone for all the departments that surround it. If Chicago fails, then we will all suffer the consequences." He continued with an impassioned appeal, "But if we succeed, the road will be open for the rest of you to stand on your rights and be heard."

Asked by one suburban representative concerning a hypothetical situation involving a fire on their border with the City, "What if the fire we're responding to turns out to be a half block inside the city limits of Chicago?" he postulated. "What are you asking, that we turn around and go back?"

The national union rep shot back immediately, standing and removing his cowboy hat for emphasis, "You're damn right I am!"

Union President Frank "Moon" Muscare quickly reacted to the grumbles that surfaced and attempted to tone down the request by re-iterating his position, that each man had to make that decision on his own. "You have to decide what you want to be," he suggested. "Do you, or don't you want to be a strike breaker?"

The union's attorney offered some explanations for those

who wanted more information. He explained that while strike-breaking tactics were prohibited by Illinois statutes, it has never been tested in a firefighters' strike. In Illinois, strikes by firefighters were prohibited by law.

Mutual Aid responses among departments must be reciprocal, he pointed out, and posed the question, "How could Chicago reciprocate if the city was in the midst of a strike?

A sketchy pact was eventually drafted at the meeting and signed by most attending. It stipulated that Mutual Aid exists for the benefit of brother firefighters when dealing with a large emergency, but that utilizing that agreement to augment reduced forces due to a strike actually constitutes "strike breaking." Additional language said that suburban departments responding into the city to cover strike related reductions would be refused such mutual aid response by others signing the agreement.

More of a solidarity pledge between union groups than a binding or legal agreement, the pact among firefighter labor representatives was sufficient to cause Chicago fire administrators to begin polling area suburban chiefs concerning their stand on mutual aid response. The union needed firefighter labor groups throughout the surrounding suburbs to unite. Chicago city administrators, on the other hand, needed suburban municipal leaders to present a unified stance as well. Some municipalities indicated that under the provisions of an existing mutual aid contract with Chicago, they would respond only if requested through proper channels. Others said they would respond to a large fire or major disaster, but would not provide station coverage. Some felt that assistance of any kind was not advisable during any labor problems. In any event, a sizable blow was dealt to the city's credibility over securing contingency promises to combat union threats.

In the suburbs, firefighters were faced with their own decisions to make. Would they in fact have to decide whether or not they would act as strike breakers? Would they suffer disciplinary actions as a result? What about the safety of firefighters responding into the city? There were no easy answers, and no precedents to follow.

Gumming up the works even more, one Local #2 vice president said after the meeting that he was not concerned about the possibility of suburban forces coming into the city. "They've never fought fires like we do," he said in an angry outburst. "They'll just stand there with their thumbs in their mouths." Of course, this wasn't well received by suburban firefighters.

Also, a threat was unofficially circulated and attributed to the union was that any suburban fire equipment responding into the city would probably not return in one piece. City Managers and Mayors now had a real concern over depriving their own communities of protection, with no guarantee that another suburb would respond in a station-coverage move up procedure. They were also understandably concerned about losing an expensive piece of equipment ($85,000 or more for an engine in 1980 dollars) at the hands of angry strikers.

The Chicago Fire Commissioner made it known that he would more than likely only request equipment for station coverage, and that direct fire response would not be needed.

One union rep pointed what he felt was a glaring ironic contradiction with the whole mutual aid concept, where neighboring fire departments respond across boundaries to assist with major fires or incidents. Referring to an existing residency requirement that all Chicago firefighters must live within the city, he wondered, "How does it happen that under a mutual aid agreement a firefighter can respond into another town and even die there, but he can't live there?" The question hit home to many firefighters, since mutual aid agreements and responses rendered the need for firefighters to live nearby no longer necessary.

Most suburban firefighters prayed that once the strike was actually called, Chicago would not call for help.

As it turned out, our department was never called on for either manpower or equipment. What I didn't know at the time, though, was that the strike would still become an intimate experience of my own.

Since the rank and file had previously voted to authorize union leadership to call a strike, the Chicago Firefighter's Union decided to do so and ordered a "walkout" at 5:15 a.m. on February 14th. St. Valentines Day already had a prominent, though infamous, place in Chicago history but this time the Valentine messages came to the city in the form of firefighters leaving their stations carrying their helmets, boots and bunker coats to join the first picket lines ever to march in front of Chicago firehouses.

I knew that their plan was to successfully pull a majority of union personnel out of every firehouse in the City of Chicago for three days -- showing solidarity and cooperation from all three duty shifts, and then return to duty with a city now more willing to talk. The union initially claimed over 80 percent walkout to which the city countered with an estimate closer to 50 percent. Many stations were virtually abandoned as total walkouts occurred throughout the city.

That was the assumption when I received a call at home

from Firehouse Magazine founder and editor Dennis Smith from New York. I had been a frequent contributor to the magazine for a couple of years by then, and the managing editor suggested that I be given the assignment. I can only imagine Smith's concern over trusting this story to a relative unknown. Smith was himself the author of the best selling book "Report From Engine Company 82", along with other books about the fire service. One of those books, "Glitter & Ash" had as its premise a firefighters' strike in a major US city. The book examined the impact of such a strike, not only on the city and the department, but on individual firefighters and the families involved on both sides of the line. This strike in neighboring Chicago had practically jumped from the pages of that book.

Smith's concern was made even more evident when he told me that he was considering jumping on a plane and coming in to cover the strike himself. As we talked, he asked questions concerning my proximity to the city but focused more on how I planned on covering this story. Having never covered anything this large, this important, or this immediate before, I could only wing it. The most telling question was when he asked me what I felt the "timbre" of the story would be. That's when I realized that just a factual reportage of the events would not be enough. I'd need to be at some of the stations, talk to the strikers and those who stayed in, and to families as well. He wanted a lot. But hey, the strike was only going to last 3 days, so I convinced him I was up to the job. As I headed downtown, I didn't know it was only the first of a 23 day ordeal.

I drafted the very first line of the eventual article in my head as I pulled up near an Uptown District Chicago fire station at Wilson and Racine and witnessed several striking firefighters in small groups on the station ramp with picket signs in hand:

"In Chicago, posters showing a picture of Mayor Jane Byrne with a target printed across her face are outselling similar posters depicting the Ayatollah Khomeini. Chants of "Burn, Witch Byrne" count the cadence for the first firefighter strike picket-line in the history of the city."

My mistake on day one was approaching striking firefighters with a large, bulky cassette tape recorder in hand and with my thin reporters' spiral notebook in the other. Many union members already felt betrayed by the press who they felt were against them. This kind of mistrust is a staple for any labor action, with the accusations of a friendly or hostile press coming usually from both sides. Here I was, a sympathetic individual attempting to objectively report a story, bringing a tape recorder to make sure I got all quotes down accurately. I might as well have pissed on their boots when I arrived.

It took a while, after getting rid of the recorder and learning to not hold my pad and pen at the ready in front of me, before I was able to talk to a few strikers and gain their trust – if only tentatively. I spent an hour or so at this, one of the busier stations in the city. Then, for contrast, I headed for the city's Cumberland station on the west side for a more suburban environment.

A heavy snow had started to fall as I walked up to the small group outside the Cumberland station. The snow was the big chunky wet kind of snow that fell in clumps and carpeted lawns and sidewalks almost immediately. Three strikers were huddled around a 50 gallon drum where scrap lumber and 2 x 4 sections burned. The glow of the fire could be seen through several ventilation holes punched into the sides. This was where the term "Brotherhood of the Barrel" was born. Not only was I able to get quotes and information from the guys around the barrel, a local and popular ward alderman arrived to shake hands and engage the press. He enthusiastically detailed his sympathy and intentions to me at great length. I didn't want to pop his bubble with the fact that I wasn't a news reporter; I let him rant.

I returned the following day to the downtown station, finding that some of the neighborhood had come out in a variety of ways to support the firefighters.

A young couple caught my eye as they were taking multiple photos from various angles, at times pulling out a light meter to check exposure. Realizing these were not just passersby, I knew that any story without photos would be incomplete, and approached them to see if I could get a print or two. I learned that they were journalism photography students and had just started a departmentally approved project photographing life in the firehouse when the strike began. We quickly struck a deal. They would receive separate payment for any photos used in my story when published. A handshake and exchange of phone numbers sealed the deal.

(When I eventually had to turn over a check to these two for the photos, I realized how important photos were to my freelancing enterprise and went out and bought a new camera. Within two weeks, I was developing and printing my own black and white photos in a temporary darkroom in a basement laundry room.)

I spent several more days dropping by firehouses after that, but also increased my contact list of union spokespeople, city sources and others as the strike ebbed and flowed. Tactics were unleashed and backfired, offers were made and rejected, meetings were held then abruptly ended. Talk shows on the radio spurred more and more angry calls, various national union leaders came and provided new sound bites, and accusations became more vicious and threatening.

A few firefighters and officers who stayed on duty remained at the firehouses for days, resting when they could. Non-striking paramedics slept on cots at local hospitals under police protection while strikers outside the fire stations chanted "C'mon out. C'mon out." The city reported that some firefighters were returning to work, but others succumbed to the chants and left to join the strikers. Some who left the station did so with tears in their eyes, as a lifetime of tradition conflicted with calls for solidarity.

One non-striking firefighter had his reasons for staying on the job in the firehouse. "The fire department is my family," he explained. "My uncle died on the job, my father is a retired fireman. I've got two brothers in the department!" Ironically, many of the striking firefighters echoed the same family history and extended fire service family as their reason for striking. Both were equally sincere.

Eventually, after nearly a month of bitter, vicious and life-changing conflict, families torn apart, and a department split into two factions that would become part of the department's personality for decades, the strike finally came to an end.

The city agreed to beef up manpower on apparatus over the next two years and to a new grievance procedure. Some representation issues were submitted to a fact finding procedure. Amnesty was provided for all strikers in return for a docking in pay. A no strike clause was agreed to.

22 people died city wide during the strike, including fire victims and emergency medical cases. Whether the strike contributed to these deaths was a question that was hotly

debated but never settled.

A few union leaders were arrested and jailed for a few days, some damage to property was reported, but eventually both sides reached enough of an agreement to end the strike after 23 days. My article for *FIREHOUSE Magazine* grew from a 4000 word report of the strike to include 3 sidebar articles I felt necessary to capture the peripheral family and mutual aid challenges along with a chronology of the strike from start to finish

Payment for the article aside, my biggest thrill was receiving another call from editor Dennis Smith who, after reading my submission, said he was so happy with the result that they were going to run the whole thing, side bars and all. I'm glad I didn't say what I was feeling at the time, but he could have kept the check after that.

See Addendum One, "*CHICAGO 1980: Anatomy of a Firefighters' Strike*"

Chapter Nineteen

On the Picket Line

Though I had tried to provide the most objective account of the strike I could for magazine publication, I found myself exploring my own gut each day of the strike. While I was sympathetic to union needs and demands, I could also understand a few of the city's equally stubborn attitudes. Fortunately for me, I was still among those who could best be described as an outside observer. Unlike striking or on-duty firefighters, officers and their families, I didn't have to live and function on either side of the emotional and sensitive divide between those who walked, and those who stayed in. In the midst of the day-to-day developments of the nearly month-long strike, I had a chance to gather impressions and observations of life on both sides of the picket line.

Normally one of the busiest in the city of Chicago, the station at Wilson and Racine Avenue, housing Engine Co. 83 and Truck Co. 22 was among the quietest the day I chose to visit. Peering out of an office window, one lonely duty officer offered the only sign of life inside a station that responds to 4,500 engine runs and 8,000 ambulance calls a year.

Outside, picket signs were carried by blue shirts and officers alike. Two experienced battalion chiefs shared cold weather, hot coffee, and pickets with rookie firefighters. There was a feeling of fatherly support between the old timers and the newcomers. "Everybody's out," noted Chief Jack McDonaugh, a 27-year veteran, who hovered over the scene as if in command of a fire. On the first day of the strike, he would detour reporters off to the side and closely monitor any and all statements made by his co-workers.

"We work together as a family, and we take care of our own. I've buried 14 personal friends already, and we're still only a number to the city," explained Chief McDonaugh.

The chief, as if to punctuate his claim of solidarity, directed me toward a tall, middle-aged firefighter standing by a fire burning in an old rusty drum. As if on protective guard duty, the man stood a few feet apart from the others, sipping coffee out of a paper cup while he surveyed the traffic passing both in the street and on the sidewalk. Battalion Chief Ray Bieschke, with 37 years on the department, was on strike with his men.

The quiet gray haired man, who everyone referred to as "The Master", briefly summed up his reasons. "We want to retain the rights that we have, and the city wants to bust up the union."

Striking firefighters marched between remote TV rigs and squad cars as passing motorists alternately honked approval or stared in disbelief at the image of firefighters on strike. The mother of a handicapped child questioned how her daughter could be assured protection in an emergency. Paramedics on the line told her they could provide service if she would bring the child to the station.

Local residents gathered and offered support to the strikers. Elderly couples stood on the sidewalk next door, and a few families with small children chatted with the strikers as the kids romped on the fire station driveway. They were all eager to support any group that countered the "establishment" they blamed for their own situation. "Wino," a ratty-haired mongrel that seemed to represent the deteriorating condition of the Chicago uptown district, also accompanied the strikers. A friendly and familiar stray to most neighbors, someone had tied a cardboard picket sign around the dogs' midsection.

Midnight on the Picket Line.

Engine Co. 11 and Truck Co. 9 sat quietly inside the station on the city's western border on Cumberland Avenue. Outside, five striking firefighters huddled around a fire, shifting their weight from one foot to another. Two inches of snow had fallen since 9 p.m. when four more officers left their nearby stations to join the strikers. Only one captain and three lieutenants remained inside the station, removed from the falling snow and increasing resentment outside.

In reference to a non-striker, one firefighter muttered, "I may be the cook, but I'll be damned if I'll ever cook for that s.o.b. again."

Inside another station, a deputy marshal lashed out at the strikers outside his station: "We've got enough men to handle the job. We're the real firemen inside the station. Those guys out picketing aren't firemen anymore."

"The problem is that we've got a mayor that doesn't care," said Mike Mahoney, a nine-year veteran firefighter and union steward, assigned to the station housing Ladder Co. 35 and

Engine Co. 76. "We've got guys here on the line that really care. If the city is gonna set up all the rules, what good is there to sit down and talk?" Thirteen days into the strike, Mahoney speculated on the vote that led to the action. "If they held another strike vote in the future, it would never be passed. When we took the vote, we didn't think she [Byrne] would be that crazy and not negotiate."

Mahoney's family was affected by the strike, as were the families of all the strikers. "I have children in the parochial school" explained Mike's wife Mary Ann.

"There were five in the religion class who were asked if their daddies were firefighters. They said 'yes' and were asked if they were on strike. They said 'yes.' The teacher proceeded to tell them that their fathers were murderers, sinners, and bad people."

Threats were even made to some of the families of non-striking firefighters. The union continually denied that they would condone any such tactics and offered protection: "If we can help in any way, we will," remarked one strike chairman on a local radio talk show. "We don't want anybody hurt. We are offering protection to any wife of a non-striker who asks. We have firefighters right here that will sit in their homes, or outside to see that nothing happens. No damage, no bodily harm."

For some strikers, information came only from the radio talk shows that periodically motivated cheers or obscenities from their listeners as city officials spoke, citizens offered opinions, or news commentators shared their own philosophies. As they listened, the picketers' expressions ranged from angry and defiant to frustrated and bewildered.

On one morning talk show, the pro-city host was

demonizing those firefighters who had walked out and accepting mostly calls from those who agreed with him. One caller, however, had made it past the call screener and asked if he could read a short piece called "I am a Firefighter" on the air. I was listening that morning at home, while having a cup of coffee in my kitchen. Hearing the title, I thought, *"That's pretty interesting. That's the title of a piece I did a year or so ago that was published in the local paper."* A week or so earlier I had provided a copy of it to one of the CFD union leaders to pass on or use as needed, then forgot about it. Once the caller began to read it, I knew the piece was the same.

"I am a firefighter!

I have entered literally hundreds of homes in this city, homes full of fire, heat and smoke, in order that lives and property may be saved.

I have seen our citizens in a myriad of indescribable states. I see the deformed and the crippled. I remove the dead parents and grandparents. I carry away the dead and dying infants.

I have cried uncontrollably when I came home.

Citizens vomit into my mouth as I try to breathe life into their bodies; I spit it out and continue my efforts.

I face temperatures that can melt the earwax in my head and burn my skin to blisters that I won't notice until I return to the station. I am overcome by smoke, heat exhaustion and injured while protecting others.

I willingly give up my Christmas Day at home with my children and eat Thanksgiving dinner with five or six firemen instead of my family. I spend each national holiday at the firehouse or on the street responding to fireworks injuries, sick overeaters and drunken fatal accidents that occur after somebody else's party.

I take special care at 3 o'clock in the morning not to use blaring horns or sirens so as to not disturb your sleep.

I know that chances are, I will have a less than 50 percent chance of surviving the year without some form of duty injury. I know that my profession will claim the lives of more fellow workers than any other occupation in the nation.

I concern myself with my pension, so that my wife and children will be provided for should I be crippled or killed protecting your property.

I maintain a personal dedication and pride in my profession, regardless of problems of internal administration.

Every two weeks, I show up for my paycheck, and I believe I have earned every damn cent."

The union version, of course, had an additional line or two calling for union solidarity or some similar message. The radio host was uncharacteristically silent for a short while, then spoke again in a soft tone.

"OK, OK," he said quietly.

"You've made a point, and we're not disputing the service that firemen provide. Maybe we all need to hear stuff like that more often. I don't know."

After a short feel-good interlude that lasted about five or ten minutes, the opinionated calls and anti-strike vitriol resumed.

Constant bombardment by rumors, press questioning, and soul-searching had its effect on strikers, but the feeling of solidarity strengthened their resolve. Most reflected on relationships, nurtured by years of living and fighting fires together, that had been possibly irreparably shattered by the strike. Those who would soon refer to themselves as the "Brotherhood of the Barrel" would be forever separate and apart from those who chose to stay on the job. As with many labor battles, such scars could remain for years.

One seven-year veteran firefighter, grabbing the sign that was hung over his torso with a heavy length of twine, summed it up this way.

"When I first saw this sign, I got a sick feeling in my stomach; When I put it on, I was scared to death."

He dropped the sign against his chest and looked away.

"Now that I'm wearing it, I feel like I just fell off a high cliff and I'm waiting to hit."

Chapter Twenty

Airline Disaster
in our Back Yard

The potential for an airliner crash had been a running theme for years for our department. We literally had the world's busiest airport located on our southern border. So close, in fact, that the local news consistently reported on the noise complaints of communities that surrounded O'Hare International Airport. Many Des Plaines residents, especially those on our south and west sides, lived under the flight paths of outgoing airline traffic flying low overhead, with some even bothered by the near constant sound of planes taxiing and throttling up before takeoff. It was commonplace for phone conversations and dinner table banter to be routinely interrupted by a loud jet passing overhead.

Most of us were used to such noise, almost to the point of not even noticing it. Sometimes we could tell if bad weather was approaching just from the change in takeoff patterns. I found that dropping off or picking up family or friends at the airport was relatively easy, since we locals knew of still existing side roads that offered quick in-and-out access to the passenger pickup areas.

The airport was a significant part of our local economy, providing an economic engine and hub for many corporate headquarters scattered throughout the Chicago area and a hub for manufacturing, air freight providers and major distribution centers in the surrounding suburbs, including Des Plaines. The tradeoff for these economic perks were the noise and traffic, along with the ominous acceptance that if and when Murphy's Law came into play, the result could be massive and tragic.

In October of 1973, several suburban departments in the area conducted large drills in preparation for such a crash. Much of the training revolved around the implementation of a still fledgling formal Mutual Aid system and an even newer EMS system designed for major medical disasters such as tornados, bus or train crashes and possible airline disasters.

The drills were the typical practice exercises common to those in emergency services, one even populated an old school bus with victims of fake injuries and scattered bodies about in a local park to allow EMS responders and local hospitals to test out new triage systems and distribution of patients to area hospitals. Like most such drills, lots of mistakes and problems popped up. But that's what these drills were for; not to do everything perfectly, but to identify areas that needed more work and planning.

Jurisdiction was one of the main areas of confusion, since the area around O'Hare International -- especially on the northern side where Des Plaines was situated -- offered a patchwork of nearby city, county and township fire district boundaries even more confusing than many political voting district maps. If you look at a map of the City of Chicago, you'll see located at approximately the 10 o'clock position an outcropping enveloping O'Hare International Airport, surrounded by various northwest suburbs. Connecting the airport and the city proper, a thin umbilical runs along either side of the Kennedy Expressway officially making the airport a part of Chicago.

On Friday, May 25, 1979, at 3:04 pm the dreaded incident finally happened.

Flight 191 from Chicago's O'Hare International Airport began as part of the Memorial Day exodus. 30 to 45 seconds after leaving the ground, the DC-10 jumbo jet with 272 passengers aboard plunged into a police canine training field just a few yards from a mobile home complex and instantly became international news and part of civil aviation history.

Within seconds, emergency lines in nearby communities were jammed. Initial reports included claims that a cargo plane had crashed into a trailer park and that a passenger plane had exploded on the highway. Ambulances from several departments, including Chicago, began streaming toward the accident. Upon arrival, fire units were immediately frustrated at the grisly realization that there were no possible survivors. A tremendous fire, fed by 72,600 gallons of aviation fuel (a full load) consumed two old hangars, a number of junked automobiles, and two mobile homes. Charred corpses were scattered in all directions. Some were piled against a chain-link fence.

Chicago Fire Department crash vehicles that responded from the airport were on the scene and began extinguishment. Fire apparatus from 36 communities arrived, and ambulances started to line up as emergency plans were put into effect at local hospitals. Comprehensive disaster plans were activated as reports were confirmed. The pressing need was for a temporary morgue.

Among those who first noticed the thick black column of smoke belching above the fireball was Des Plaines Engine 62, several blocks east of the incident. Elk Grove Township Ambulance 321, less than a half mile to the west, radioed back to headquarters that they were going to investigate. At the same time, Elk Grove Village Engine 118 pushed out of its house after sighting the explosion.

Emergency lines to fire and police departments were flooded with calls. Reports varied with each caller, "A building or something just exploded," said one caller. An operator-assisted call rambled about a fire "just behind the house." All radio frequencies became overloaded with hurried instructions. Voice communications were drowned out by sirens and air horns. Civilian excitement was tempered by professional calm as the grim report crept into conflict-filled airways: "A report of a DC-10 crash on Touhy Avenue." With this confirmation began the multi-department response to the site of the worst single civilian airline disaster in US history.

Des Plaines Engine 62 spiraled its way around a Chicago police canine training facility just off Touhy Avenue, a few hundred yards from the end of Runway 32R. Directly behind them came five Chicago Fire airport crash trucks with men from Crash Station #2 who told me they ran for their rigs when they saw the DC-10's left engine hit the runway.

From the west, responding equipment headed for the western edge of a trailer park that had been affected, and began fighting fires that gutted one mobile home. After a burning section of fuselage had smashed into the rear of the trailer, the elderly residents were quickly carried out by neighbors. Aviation fuel spread over several acres, leaving burning pools six to eight inches deep. These fires were extinguished with massive foam delivery from Chicago fire crash trucks and an Elk Grove Township truck. Later, firefighters found the leather strap holding one of the engines' turret nozzle guns atop the Elk Grove Township truck burned to a crisp.

Chemicals spewed from the crash vehicles. Firefighters advanced with headlines from booster tanks and tankers until relays could be established for a supply line. 60 to 70 percent of the fuel fire was knocked down by the crash trucks using Aqueous Film Foaming Foam, which extinguishes flammable liquid fires and provides a surface coating over the spilled fuel that reduces or prevents the likelihood that fumes might suddenly re-ignite. Some spot fires and stubborn pockets were soon recognized as bodies still burning. Molten metals from the aircraft, two old hangars, and junked automobiles intermingled with each other in the midst of the thick black smoke.

The Elk Grove Fire Chief called for a mutual aid box alarm, calling for help from surrounding cities and communities. MABAS (Mutual Aid Box Alarm System) Central in Arlington Heights took control over all mutual aid radio traffic and response. Units arriving from all directions were deployed to provide hose line relays from two distant hydrants, one located off a well at the rear of the trailer park and the other nearly a half mile down the highway. Ambulances were staged, half facing east and half facing west, with police keeping traffic lanes open for their expected race to local hospitals.

Although hospitals were notified to activate their disaster plans, the reality became quickly apparent to those on the scene: there would be no survivors from the plane itself. Elk

Grove ambulances treated, then transported, two victims from an old converted hangar drenched in burning aviation fuel. Two others died within the structures involved.

The response was massive as thirty-five surrounding suburbs responded. The suburban mutual aid system provided for move-up assignments to cover communities that sent equipment to the crash site, and Chicago sent 12 engines, 4 aerial ladders, a snorkel, a flying squad, 2 helicopters, and 6 ambulances, in addition to 5 crash vehicles from the airport. Fire department command was handed off and moved around the scene as the situation required. One chief was in charge of water supply, one of staging ambulances, and another of supervising extinguishment. Police command centers were established at several points around the area to keep away onlookers and looters. Local news helicopters, competing overhead for a good camera position, had to be waved off since the force of their propellers pushed thick black smoke back down on the responders.

Ambulances arrived from miles away only to be staged on the sidelines. Firefighters, EMTs, paramedics, and other medical personnel, searching for survivors, walked among the hundreds of charred and dismembered passengers, covering them with plastic sheets and pounding stakes into the ground nearby to mark their location for body part recovery operations soon to follow.

Within 20 minutes of the crash, the message was sent that no additional ambulances were needed. A request was made for more body bags and stakes. Three hours after the crash, remains were being transported to a temporary morgue set up in an American Airlines hangar at O'Hare. The crash site was unceremoniously placed in the hands of the medical examiner and the Federal Aviation Administration (FAA), while thousands of feet of hose were rolled and stacked on engine tailboards.

Everyone who participated in the disaster shared one common thought: it can happen again. The consensus was that the operation actually went smoother than expected. Even with the short-lived problem of jurisdiction, 36 responding departments worked together quickly and effectively. Extinguishment was rapid, response was immediate, and the expected jurisdictional battles were minimal. In most cases, any conflicts were after the fact. Criticism was generally constructive, with many of the recommendations similar to those that followed practice drills held a few years earlier.

Difficulty in communications was the first problem that confronted all who responded. The first responding units were originally operating on their own local frequencies. Since there were so many different departments in the suburban area, the frequencies were divided among several of them.

Eight minutes into the emergency, the box alarm was called for, and units began to switch over from one frequency to another designated for fireground operations. Still, chief officers responding were forced to switch periodically to their own local or administrative frequencies to get messages through. At times, orders were repeated several times over several frequencies before they were received. It was found that not all fire apparatus was equipped with the NIFERN (Northern Illinois Fire Emergency Radio Network) frequency. Some police units did not have the equivalent of NIFERN called ISPERN (Illinois State Police Emergency Radio Network), so the communication problem overlapped between all departments, causing some communication challenges to establishing a plan of action.

Thirty-six different fire departments were represented at

the scene in various strengths. In addition to several suburban and Chicago police vehicles, the Illinois State Police, the Cook County Sheriff's office, Civil Defense (now referred to as Emergency Management Agency), the Red Cross, airport authorities, the FAA, medical examiners, and other agencies were all on scene. Some 507 fire and 398 police personnel responded, engulfing the site in radio traffic and flooding the available VHF and UHF bands. The weight of all this radio traffic caused so much radio interference that the first paramedics on the scene found it nearly impossible to use their telemetry equipment.

The command structure over all these departments was established as the situation demanded. The jurisdiction question was resolved after Elk Grove Village initiated a box alarm. At that point, command was further divided by need (extinguishment, water supply, equipment, manpower deployment, and medical). This "coalition" of command worked well, possibly because the area of involvement was uncharacteristically tight and compact. The aircraft had crashed at a slow speed; it fell almost straight down and from a relatively low height. Also, with a relatively small debris area, it was apparent early in the operation that there were no survivors. And with the concern of rescue, treatment, and transportation of the injured tragically unnecessary, more attention could be directed to the containment and extinguishment of the fires.

Chicago crash trucks were equipped with foam, and suburban apparatus had only the water that their booster tanks contained. The closest hydrants were 1,500, 4,000, 4,500 feet away, and caused delays in setting a supply line for the handlines. Tankers were summoned for immediate water supply as relays were being set up. Some firefighters on the scene suggested that several more tankers should be included in the first response to an airliner crash, providing more water from the start while hydrants were located and relays set. In this case, 19 engines were set in series - connected by feeder lines, pumping one to another -- from three different hydrants.

Over-response is often considered an unwritten rule within the fire service. The logic often proves to be the difference between a "save" and a loss on occasion. It is easier to send back unneeded equipment than to call for it later. Within the first minute of the crash, fire and police units descended on the site from all directions. Not until a command structure was established was there a possibility to limit the manpower or equipment responding. No definite plan, other than a special ambulance box, had been arranged for such an incident. The Mutual Aid Box Alarm System had been designed to deal primarily with large structure fires.

An airliner crash occurring well within an established protection district boundary offers more control capability for command personnel. They can be more selective in equipment response. Flight 191, however, went down in an area where first reports gave several locations, all near a point joining several different protection districts. The Chicago Fire Department implemented its own Disaster Plan, which called for private ambulances to be dispatched on incidents involving 30 or more injured persons. Many suburban departments dispatched equipment at will, before and after the mutual aid box alarm was called.

The end result forced many firefighters, medical teams, and other rescue personnel to be staged on the sidelines, looking on while others performed assigned tasks. Police response was so heavy that some had difficulty getting through the sea of squad cars. The press and news media equipment were restricted outside a roped-off perimeter. Local hospitals sent medical teams in vain. Buses were sent from the airport to transport walking injured, and doctors who were passing by stopped to offer assistance. All the well-intentioned people who descended on the site eventually formed a multitude of frustrated onlookers, resigned to the fact that their skills were not needed.

Even with the few problems that surfaced, all agreed that confusion was at a minimum, cooperation was enthusiastic, and the instinctive fire service tradition of teamwork prevailed to produce a well-organized operation. As in any emergency operation, many came away with suggestions concerning the next disaster. But everyone prayed that day would never come.

Chapter Twenty-One

Air Crash Aftermath: Between Laughter and Tears

Everyone who responded to the Flight 191 crash had a story. Some shared them immediately with others, some only with co-responders. Some kept their experiences to themselves, while others shared to the point of irritation recounting visuals and experiences ad-nauseam. Others would actually leave the room whenever the incident was discussed in depth. There was no template at the time for post-disaster debriefing beyond the areas of basic response, equipment and fire ground SOP's. At least not for us, who at the time could only read of such programs still in their infancy elsewhere.

First responders told of their individual experiences as they arrived on the scene, some descriptions more graphic than others. Other responders recalled images in short mental flashes or merely as glimpses through massive amounts of smoke and steam: a large field of still burning or smoldering debris, body parts scattered among pools of aviation fuel.

One paramedic was haunted for years by a solitary image

of a victim's head. It had come to rest in the area of an old hanger used for vehicle and junk storage. The head was wedged under the front of a taxicab tire; the eyes were still wide open and seem to stare surrealistically at a small pile of fresh strawberries -- spilled from an on-board food container -- just a foot and a half away.

Others remember moving through the smoke and steam with hand lines, climbing occasionally over what they thought was debris only to realize, as the smoke cleared, they were actually walking over charred human torsos. Some remembered the sporadic and muffled popping sounds that later were determined to be skulls breaking under the pressure of brain matter expanding in the surrounding heat. The relatively small crash site yielded more than enough horror stories to fuel many individual nightmares for years to come.

The damage was complete and devastating. The airliner had nose-dived with a full load of fuel into a field. Its left wing tip had first dug into the ground, leaving a long trench pointing to where the fuselage nosed into the ground. The destruction was total, and death was instantaneous for everyone aboard. For many, the impact turned seat belts into beltline guillotines, quickly separating torsos from legs. The massive jet fuel explosion added to the fragmentation and spreading of bodies and body parts. One of the more iconic visual images of the event was the eventual sea of small orange banner flags scattered throughout the crash scene. Each banner marked the location of a body part.

This 1979 crash occurred before most of the post-traumatic debriefing and counseling procedures had been developed for first responders. Without any existing guidelines or suggestions on how to deal with this level of carnage, the firefighters who responded to the plane crash quickly fell into the long-established practice of minimizing the horrors and depth of tragedy. This was a common tactic and practice among firefighters and was the same as that used by combat veterans, police officers and others commonly exposed to such sights. Minimize, deflect, ignore, or in many cases, make a joke to diffuse.

Our shift had a couple of newer recruits, also referred to as "probies" or "new boots", one of whom was still a bit sensitive at the time to the sight of blood and other gory visuals he encountered on calls. His sensitivities weren't enough to impair his performance and would soon dissipate through experience and continual exposure. Still, at the firehouse, he was a prime target for a merciless crew always willing to capitalize on a perceived weakness. It sounds cruel, but within the total context of how first-responders bond and solidify as a team, it was just another formative day at the firehouse.

One Sunday soon after the crash, the shift cook had grilled barbecued chicken in the back of the fire station. Before bringing in a large tray full of an assortment of legs, wings, breasts and thighs, some blackened with barbeque sauce, one of the guys placed on each piece a toothpick with a small orange banner attached – which had been cut out of construction paper earlier - emulating the crash scene just days before.

As the tray was brought into the kitchen it was met with a few nervous laughs, some groans and "you gotta be kidding" responses. One firefighter jumped up and tried to pull off the toothpicks even before the tray touched the table.

"For Chrissakes, give us break, ok?" he said tossing the toothpicks into the trash.

But the joke had already been played, everyone eventually had a great laugh The probie was one more step toward becoming a more integral part of the team. Unfortunately, the prank was to become an embarrassing bell that could not be subsequently un-rung.

Firehouse humor following tragic events is a common release mechanism, and has been a staple coping mechanism used for decades by those who share these kinds of ugly and gory experiences. Firehouse humor isn't always understood by outsiders who rarely if ever are exposed to this kind of coping mechanism. Modern counseling and support systems may have been developed by then, but PTSD, or Post Traumatic Stress Disorder, was not a familiar term in the days following the Flight 191 crash. Most firefighters were left to their own traditional coping tactics: But the jokes didn't stay in the firehouse this time.

In 1979, unlike today when sound recordings or cellphone videos would be shared on social media or worse, all that was needed was someone making mention of it at a local tavern, which eventually led to a couple of angry letters to the local editor accusing firefighters of not respecting those who had died. How dare these firefighters engage in black humor when so many were suffering losses and tragic memories, the letters said.

I was approached by several firefighters with a copy of one of those letters. As the resident firehouse "letter writer" I was asked to craft a defensive response to this expressed outrage. I shared the firefighters' concerns, so instead of attempting to deny the accusations, I wrote the following op-ed which was printed in the local weekly newspaper.

"In Monday's paper, a firefighter was loosely quoted as saying some of the firefighters who returned to the station after

the crash of Flight 191 engaged in what some refer to as "black humor", and by doing so showed disrespect to those who died.

The uncomfortable jokes that may overcome firemen at the worst possible times are more than a macabre sense of humor, and do not represent a lack of respect for the dead. They serve as a relief vale for individuals who witness and deal with death on a different level than do many doctors, funeral directors or family and friends at the wake or funeral of a loved one.

For most people, death is the guy on TV who bites the dust clutching a bloodless chest after a .45 caliber automatic has just exploded inches away. Or it's the seemingly restful individual laid out in a coffin, wearing makeup and a suit looking "... so natural you can almost see him breathe." For most firemen and other early responders, death is a much uglier reality.

Death can be the child who cannot be revived after being pulled from a backyard swimming pool or the 24 year-old girl whose brains are splashed all over the windshield of a car. Death is the terminal cancer patient who, though just 45 years old, looked over 90, half eaten away after lying on the floor between a toilet and the wall for the past month and a half. For firefighters, as well as police and rescue personnel, death is a visually ugly assault on the integrity of human existence. It smells, rots, decays and is never attractive, much less funny.

A firefighters' reaction to a specific situation is a different matter. Were every DOA or lost patient allowed to affect a firefighter, the job of saving lives could not be accomplished. Emotions have to be vented or the psychological boiler will explode. No firefighter completes his career without tears, however, as the sheer weight of certain tragedies is occasionally too much for even the strongest individual to bear.

The inclination to joke, after a situation that should

normally generate somberness and grief is a clearly made decision to help clear yet another emotional hurdle. Laughter and tears, we learn eventually, coexist on either side of an extremely thin membrane. Stress can violate that dividing line and the two reactions of grief and humor at times bleed into each other.

Whichever way the emotion is vented, the end result is relief, and both serve as an overload preventer of a kind, allowing those who serve a path to continue serving the very next day."

At the time, I was still preparing a comprehensive article on the crash and response for *FIREHOUSE Magazine*, and literally had become a listening post for several firefighters and officers, each with a unique recurring image and point of view. So the words flowed freely as I typed the letter and it was easy to write; much of it had already been bouncing around in my head since the crash. I don't know if the civilian complaints continued, but at least no more angry letters surfaced in the local press.

Chapter Twenty-Two

The Garbage House

My older brother Bob was still on the police department in the summer of 1974, and we would occasionally run into each other on an official call. One such opportunity found us both, if only for 10 seconds or so, featured on national TV.

I was in the middle of a nearly three month stretch as Acting Lieutenant on our west side station's Engine 63. As a company officer, it was important to get a rundown, however brief or seemingly insignificant, on the previous shift's activities, any problems with equipment or other information. One particular morning I learned that angry neighbors in a row of townhouses off of Oakton Street had been calling in false alarms.

"There's a townhouse that the neighbors say is stinking up the whole neighborhood," explained the lieutenant who was going off duty." Apparently it's vacant, and they think the city is blowing them off, so they were getting all worked up and started calling in alarms to make a big issue and get someone out there."

Complaints were ranging from bad odors coming from the property to a more curious claim that some green "ooze" was actually coming out from under the baseboards of a common wall.

"You might want to spin by there with the engine and spot the hydrants in case somebody decides to torch the place," he suggested, having already logged in two false calls to the address he handed to me.

We had hardly completed our morning vehicle and equipment check when the alarm came in for that same address.

"Code three, report of a structure fire at 259-J West Dover Drive," came the clearly articulated voice over the speakers, with a slight "here we go again" inflection. "Police are on the scene stating no fire or smoke showing."

We headed for our rigs, without even finishing our morning equipment inventory.

A code three response for a possible structure fire required a response by at least two engines, a ladder truck and an MICU along with a shift commander. As the first engine in, we pulled up on the scene and I could see a yard full of civilians, a few police squad cars and two Chicago based TV news trucks, already with their mobile transmission towers extended high over the roof tops. A crowd had formed around a tall, red-haired fellow in a suit who I recognized as the state's lieutenant governor. Standing on the front stoop of the townhouse was my brother Bob, first giving me a high sign as our engine pulled up, then signaling a "waive off" to let me know there was no real emergency.

We pulled up near the sidewalk, and I grabbed my portable radio and met him on the front step.

"No fire here," he said, looking first left, then right as he spoke, his with his hands anchored to his belt by his thumbs.

"The natives already got the Lt. Governor here, and I guess they wanted to make everything more interesting for the TV guys."

He was clearly not entertained by the growing circus. I radioed in that there was no fire and to return all responding units. Later that day, our Mother was be thrilled to watch the evening news and see one of her sons in full firefighting gear get out of an engine and join her oldest son on the steps of that townhouse, her eldest son's badge and sergeant stripes catching the sunlight just right. It was our 15 seconds of fame.

Bob explained that the day before he had entered the townhouse and arrested the occupant, who had been sitting in his living room atop a pile of garbage while eating a home delivery pizza. The neighbors were at high alert and at peak frustration level as they demanded more action by the city health or building departments.

"Wanna have a look around?" he said to me, pulling open the outer screen door.

I signaled for the guys on the engine to join us, telling them to be sure and wear boots and gloves. Bob had to push in on the entry door against a then unseen barrier to allow enough of an opening for us to squeeze through.

I learned that seven years before an argument over who would take out the garbage or possibly a dispute with the garbage bill resulted in nobody taking out the garbage at all. Ever. As three galvanized steel trash cans stood empty outside near the backdoor filled only with cobwebs, the family kept filling garbage and trash bags and stuffing them where ever they could find space.

We actually had to climb up about one and half to two feet after pushing open the front door, which revealed the only small wedge of floor space visible in the entire house. We then found ourselves walking on a surface made up of paper wrappings, dried food remains and stains, and who knows what else. Over time, much of the surface had dried and become an encrusted layer which, when stepped on and broken, released the stench and stink of rotting materials beneath. All the furniture, save for a couple of folding chairs here and there, was covered with trash or trash bags. This sometimes two to three foot layer of garbage and trash extended everywhere throughout the entire first floor.

Closets were filled from top to bottom with filled trash bags. To check the upstairs, we had to climb a continuing layer of garbage all the way to the second level. No stairs were visible, so for each step I had to dig in my boot a bit into the trash to gain a foothold.

Upstairs revealed even more disgusting images, especially in the bathrooms. None of the toilets in the unit were working, having backed up a year or so before. Dried fecal matter and toilet paper filled the bowls. In two of the bathrooms, the toilets had overflowed onto the floor with a pile of paper and organic matter beginning to stack up in the corner behind the toilet.

Walk-in closets were filled with garbage bags to the ceiling. In the master bedroom, instead of a box spring, one queen sized mattress rested on top of at least 2 feet of debris.

As the garbage got higher than the top of the mattress, Bob explained, they would pick up the mattress, kick all the crap under the mattress and then set it down again.

The basement was practically full. We had barely enough room to climb down another descending slope of solid garbage which also hid the stairs. We had to crouch low since the trash level was so high. The further we crept down and into the basement, the more shallow the trash level became, but still no floor space was visible. There were were no basement windows and any light bulbs in place probably burned out years earlier so we needed flashlights to navigate as if we had been exploring a subterranean cave. Then I felt something move quickly across my right boot.

"Holy crap," yelled Stu Merton, another firefighter, following close behind me as he jerked back and away.

"Did you see the size of that?"

"What? Where!" I shot back, as my flashlight beam quickly crossed the now rapid and frantically searching beams from both his flashlight and Bob's.

"I felt it, but didn't see it!"

"That had to be the biggest rat I've ever seen," Merton said. "It had to be this long not including the tail," holding out his gloved hands about a foot apart.

Our basement tour ended then and there, and we worked our way back up to the main floor and out the front door.

The townhouse owner, I found out later, was a local butcher; wife was a nurse at a local hospital. They had two kids and the entire family had lived in the house during most of the previous seven years or so as the garbage piles grew until they nearly became part of the structure. The couple had divorced several months ago, and the husband now lived there alone, ignoring the growing number of health department inquiries resulting from the angry calls of his neighbors.

Those living in adjacent townhouse units had become increasingly aware of a foul odor in their neighborhood. It was eventually determined to be coming from the butcher's townhouse. It took an arrest warrant issued the day before we pulled up to ascertain the source of the smell and reason for the green material oozing through at least one wall.

After the politicians expressed their outrage and concern on camera, and the TV crews had packed up their equipment and left, a public works crew was called in along with what seemed like an endless parade of dumpsters to begin the task of mitigating the growing public health problem. As soon as the first crew, each dressed head to foot in protective vinyl suits, began removing the first few shovels of debris, the putrid stench became much, much worse. The odor became so bad that operations were halted until each crew member could be equipped with breathing apparatus.

We never had to respond again after that day. It took nearly a year, after clearing the property and nearly gutting the entire unit structurally, before the townhouse was again habitable. At the time, in the mid-1970's, this type of call was rare enough to become a national news clip for a day or two. These days, such properties have become the focus of at least one reality series on cable TV.

It proved without a doubt, however, that shouting "Fire" gets a lot more attention than shouting "garbage".

Chapter Twenty-Three

Brave and Fearless: Or Just One-Eyed Men?

One of the duties of those firefighters with the least time on the job is that of helping to conduct firehouse tours. Rookies are asked to tag along so they can learn how to handle a variety of questions from visitors. When I first helped out one of the more veteran firefighters, I quickly found that I looked forward to these opportunities rather than dreaded them as so many others did.

The main common denominator between tours for kids and tours for adults was the amount of myths and innaccurate perceptions that many had about the fire service and firefighters themselves. One way I would open up an opportunity to dispel some of those misconceptions, was to initially announce, "Good morning everyone, I'm Firefighter Rick, and I'm the one that's responsible for checking for dirty underwear." Since just about everyone can remember their mom justifying her rule to be sure and put on clean underwear "….in case you're in an accident", I had everyone's attention and could explain some other inaccurate perceptions as well.

Fire service and firefighter myths abound, and there's no way to list and debunk all of them here. Most are the result of how little most people know about the fire service, firefighting, or that mystic place called the "firehouse". One common belief is that all firefighters do is sit around the firehouse, either whittling away on a stick in front of the station, or playing checkers as the trusty station Dalmation sits at their feet. As talented as Norman Rockwell was, some of his paintings and prints of firehouse life in Americana – several of which grace my own walls at home –may have helped perpetuate some of these misconceptions. (Some of these myths were covered earlier in "Planet Firehouse".)

Many people believe, at varying degrees, that all firefighters are heros, brave and unselfish, fearless, and willing to sacrifice their lives to protect the public they serve. Fortunately this belief can be helpful when it's time to ask for a salary raise or additional benefits, but it can be unfortunate when the expectations of citizens – or fire victims – exceed what firefighters can do, can't do, will do, or won't do.

I don't believe that firefighters individually think they are any braver than any other segment of our society. Firefighters that bask under any self appointed label of "fearless", on the other hand, could be better described as inexperienced or just plain stupid.

What separates firefighters from others is merely a balanced result of training, equipment, experience, and common sense. This balance isn't included along with the firefighter's initial issue of boots, turnout gear, and helmets, but is a cumulative result of initial training, fireground experience and the example set by other more seasoned firefighters. It is also nurtured by the firefighters' collective ability to recognize and accept their own weaknesses and vulnerabilities along with their own individual strengths.

A well honed firefighting company has come to know each other's strengths and weaknesses, and instinctively draws on individual strengths while at the same time compensating for shortcomings. One firefighter may possess the initial strength and nearly unstoppable force to make a rapid and effective entry while at the nozzle of a hoseline and can quickly push deeper into a structure to find the seat of the fire or make a difficult rescue. After that near explosive and rapid effort, however, he is quickly drained and needs to be rested. Other firefighters might not be the first in, but prove to have the extra stamina needed to perform the tiring and exhaustive tasks of ripping open walls, ceilings, and door jams helping to seek out extensions of the fire and preventing a rekindle. Most fire companies learn this balance and use it to their benefit.

Serving as an acting company officer on many emergency calls and fires, I quickly accepted that others in my company – many of them working as carpenters, electricians or in other trades – could literally look at some stuctures with an educated x-ray vision of sorts. Though basic building construction is a significant part of firefighter training, unlike me, they could look at a structure and know exactly what was behind the walls, where there were load bearing supports, potentially dangerous wiring or where natural gas lines were hidden. It would have been arrogant, stupid, and dangerous to not heed their input.

Firefighter deaths and injuries are usually a surprise. When a new recruit takes the oath, they realize that there are potential hazards such as flames, structural collapse, toxic smoke, falling debris, and explosions and that much of their training will be directed toward recognizing and avoiding such hazards when possible. Annual statistics change, but National Fire Protection Agency (NFPA) records show that yearly firefighter deaths have significantly dropped. In 2010, for example, they were less than a third of what they were in 1981, when such statistics began to be collected nationwide. Much of this drop is due to more standardized training, improved firefighting gear and equipment, more sprinkler systems, and better application and enforcement of fire codes nationally.

Many fireground deaths – those fatalities that occur while fighting fires – occur in multiples, such as when a floor, wall, or ceiling collapses taking out an entire fire company. Always tragic, most of these multiple deaths were either unpredictable or follow an intensive interior search for victims -- including for homeless vagrants that may be living in abandoned buildings. The worst such incident is the tragic 9-11 attack and collapse of the twin towers in 2001 which killed 343 New York City firefighters, becoming the largest incident of fireground deaths of firefighters in history. Each year more deaths are attributable to fireground, rescue and recovery activities, responding to and from calls and training accidents.

Personally, over my 26 years, I remember being scared a lot, as are many firefighters. In most cases, that fear becomes an unavoidable reminder to focus, evaluate, assess, and act. When that fear turns into panic, no amount of training can help. The most important result of comprehensive training and experience, then, is knowing when the line between fear and panic is being approached, recognizing that it's there, and either keeping it at arm's length or getting the hell out of the situation. Once you've felt panic, it's not hard to recognize.

My first time approaching that line was early in my career, at a residential fire. We responded to a delayed alarm at a single story ranch home with smoke coming from the upstairs windows. Seventeen or so firefighters arrived on scene with our typical Code 3 response of two engines, a ladder truck and an ambulance, yet there were still only 3 or 4 airpacks available. I found myself along with two other firefighters making entry through the front door to search for possible victims. I quickly became separated from the others in the living room which was rapidly filling with rolling hot and black smoke, slowly stacking from the ceiling down. I learned later that I had merely turned right when the other two turned left. I found myself on the other side of a large cabinet which I mistook in the now blinding smoke for an interior wall.

Finding myself alone, I called out a few times. but I knew that it was unlikely that anyone would hear me over the cacophony of breaking glass, water blasting elsewhere from a two and a half inch line, and engine pumps running at full revolutions just yards away outside in front of the house. I was still on my feet, but stooping low as the smoke continued to stack down making breathing more difficult. I dropped further down to my knees, still reaching wildly in all directions to find a wall, a door, or a window.

I could feel my apprehension begin to ratchet up and then begin morphing into outright blind panic. I dropped to my belly, still moving ahead in what I thought was the direction I had come. Breathing was becoming more difficult and painful; the smoke began to choke off my trachea and it felt like hot razor blades had been forced down my gullet. I bent my head forward trying to bury my nose and mouth under my turnout coat and my shirt underneath it. *Oh my God*, I thought to myself. *I'm not gonna get out of here.*

Then I either felt or heard something like a pitiful whimper, just on the verge of that cry that immediately precedes an all out scream. At the same time my right hand made contact with what felt like a window jam. Though it was odd to find a window jam that close to the floor, I moved toward it and saw that I had reached the small horizontal window immediately under the living room's front picture window. I could hear the activity just outside, but was unable to yell out at all by this time due to the smoke. The whimper I felt seconds before started again.

I could tell that I was close to losing it. I also knew that if I did, they'd find me later, dead from smoke exhaustion or worse. With my right hand I grabbed my helmet and started hitting the window glass. I didn't think I could break the glass, but I hoped that maybe someone outside would hear me. As I repositioned myself to take a few more forceful and louder whacks at the window, my left hand felt something strangely familiar. It was a small hand crank.

I knew right away what it was and instinctively began cranking the little lever which tilted the small outside window up a bit allowing some air to come in through the small screen. The inside air pressure was competing with a slight wind just outside the tiny window, but I could feel cooler outside air against my face. I practically jammed my entire face into that window sideways, tearing part of the screen open with my nose. After a quick gulp or two of air I started hollering for help. Within a minute, I heard the sounds of two firefighters, and the unmistakeable sounds of the mechanical airpack pressure valve alternately opening and closing getting closer. They found me and guided me outside. I was transported to the hospital in the ambulance sitting upright in the back with 3 others who had also taken too much smoke.

This time I had consciously kept myself from crossing the line between defensive apprehension and all out panic. Actually, that little window handle did more to save me than any self control. Either way, had I crossed over I would have been able to make only one or two futile attempts at taking a breath before dying on the spot. I learned then that it is sometimes possible to recognize the fear for what it is, act defensively, and not let it take over.

After we were examined at the hospital, all of us except one were released immediately and returned to duty. One signficant positive result of this whole experience was an increased discussion about having more airpacks available for responding firefighters.

So, are firefighters brave? Maybe so, maybe not. There's an old saying that suggests "In the land of the blind, the one-eyed man is King." So much depends on the level of training and experience a firefighter has along with his own perception of the potential hazards. Some may act rather than retreat to not appear frightened in front of their peers. Others might become so focused on a goal or objective – especially when lives are at stake – that they may be seeing the situation through blinders that prevent them from noting or reacting to obvious dangers. Still others might have too much confidence in their own "Superman Suit" to hold them back. Of course, some may actually be just plain heroes, but they would be the last ones to actually claim the title.

A seasoned firefighter training officer once said, "Firefighters don't have to prove they are heroes. They proved that when they first raised thier hands to take the oath." A firefighter's bravery might only be a willingness to face forces that are partially understood and may not be predictable, but knowing all the time that those forces can bite them in the ass at any time.

Chapter Twenty-Four

That Was Then, and This Is Now

The fire service certainly evolved and changed during my 26 years, perhaps including some of the most significant improvements in the history of the occupation. When I retired in 1996, I felt the department had already started to outdate me in several areas. The internet and online explosion was in high gear, and even more high tech tools were being adopted or tested by fire departments nationwide.

In my last year on the job, for example, I had the opportunity to use and help evaluate a new thermal imaging camera device. The large camera had a screen about 5 or 6 inches across, surrounded by a cowl or collar that – once pressed against your face – would offer a clear thermal image of whatever you pointed at. Designed to help locate hotspots and even the familiar outline of possible victims, the new equipment promised to be a boon to both firefighting and rescue operations. Such devices are now standard equipment on some fire apparatus.

I went back to one of my old fire stations to get an overview of some of the changes that were made after I left, and was pleasantly surprised by the leaps and bounds the department had made in areas of emergency response and firefighter safety.

Each responding MICU, engine, ladder truck or other emergency vehicle is now equipped with onboard computers, linking each unit to comprehensive GPS-supported mapping systems. In addition to a constant link to dispatch operations which keep track of response times and locations, responders can instantly access information related to thier destination, such as precise address and location of residential calls, previously recorded warnings or cautions and even spot-on locations of the nearest fire hydrant. Cautions might include, for some residential addresses, whether the occupant had been involved in previous calls, whether with fire or police, if there were known guns on the premises, or special notations provided by property owners or residents concering special health or physical challenges.

As part of a department and system wide linkage, responders have access to industrial hazard information, data bases on hazardous materials handling, and other essential information gathered and input earlier – an on-going process, by the way.

Fire engines, driven and operated by trained engineers skilled and practiced in determining the proper water flow and pressure to make front line fire hose nozzles deliver water efficiently, now have onboard computers to assist in detecting and setting the proper pressure almost instantly. Ladder trucks, also serving to transport most rescue equipment to a fire scene or vehicle accident, were upgraded along with some basic rescue tools. The "Jaws of Life", once a heavy generator powered and hydraulic fluid operated prying and cutting tool, are now an intregal part of the truck. Instead of hauling the heavy generator and several yards of hydraulic hose to where it was needed, everything is mounted inside one massive cabinet. Simply slide out the generator, and pull on one of two large mounted reels which feed 100 feet or so of hydraulic hose to where ever the jaws are needed. Fast, efficient, and much easier on firefighters' backs.

Personal breathing apparatus is largely unchanged, but thier accessories keep improving. "Buddy breathing", is where one firefighter will supply air to another whose air supply has been depleted. Previously a somewhat awkward system of attaching one short length of breathing hose to a small connector on another unit, the process now provides a separate hose of around three feet that allows two firefighters to comfortably share a single tank. Motion sensitive detectors are attached to a breathing tank strap that activate and emit a loud alarm should the wearer become motionless or immobile for a preset amount of time. Some face masks, I'm told, have up front displays inside the faceplate that project the levels of remaining compressed air left in the tank, and may also include the actual temperature of the air in the firefighter's immediate proximity.

I learned that training requirements changed a great deal – and much more than I could have imagined. When I left in 1996, firefighters coming on the job were required to successfully complete training and maintain certification as paramedics. It was a basic condition of employment. This was in addition to attending a regional fire academy for several weeks, and attaining full Firefighter Certification.

Now, before the department will even accept an application, applicants must have already attained full paramedic certification, and served several months internship in that capacity. In addition, applicants must have previously attained full Firefighter certification. In short, costs for the extensive training are now borne by the applicant rather than the municipality. Once hired, recruits attend a five week regional fire training academy before eventual assignment to a shift. What was once literally a four week process to get on the job for me in 1971, is now a one year or more commitment *even before being considered for employment.*

Each engine and truck is now also a fully equipped Advanced Life Support (ALS) response unit. Each carry essential drugs, equipment and telemetry identical to that carried on the MICU, allowing each rig the ability to respond and help stabilize a patient until transport can be provided.

Naturally, firefighters themselves have also evolved and changed along with new technologies, new social patterns, and continued improvements that result from ongoing experience and new ideas. I'm glad I made that visit to specifically take note of the changes that had occured in the approximately 16 years since my last emergency response.

Leaving the station, though, I remembered what one old veteran firefighter named "Willie" told me almost 40 years earlier while standing in nearly the same spot after we'd all been shown some new piece of equipment or learned some newly established SOP. Summing it all up, he reminded me in a very loud but ever so slight Irish brogue.

"Y'know, it still all comes down to one thing," he said as we headed back into the dayroom for a cup of coffee.

"What's that?" I said, taking the bait.

"No matter what, young man," he replied, "It still comes down to puttin' the wet stuff on the red stuff!"

Some things will never change.

Epilogue

No look back by any firefighter would be complete without a special personal note concerning 9-11.

Recalling the horrors of September 11, 2001 and the loss of so many firefighters and first responders among the nearly 3,000 who perished, I'm troubled to see how the event itself seems to have dimmed in the collective memories of many in this country. Just within the past few years, some TV pundits go as far as saying we all "over-reacted" to the event. Some municipalities are now either "scaling back" or eliminating observances on that date altogether.

I finally had the opportunity to visit Ground Zero in New York in 2011. Though the new memorial was still under construction, for many firefighters, including retired members like myself, such a visit continues to be our own "pilgrimage to Mecca" -- forgive the ironic metaphor -- to show respect for the fallen. I was as surprised as my grown son who was with me was when I was unexpectedly moved to tears at one point viewing a display case showing the hundreds of patches from Police and Fire units from around the world. It epitomized and drove home the sense of brotherhood and family that first responders share, and how the survivors continue to honor their memory and ultimate sacrifice.

For me, every day after September 11, 2001 is September 12th. I hope that instead of allowing the date to diminish in importance, dissolve through historical revisions, or depreciate in patriotic value, that we will continue to honor those who responded and those who perished during this attack on America and modern civilization as we know it.

Addendum 1

CHICAGO 1980: Anatomy of a Firefighters' Strike

Published, *FIREHOUSE Magazine*, May, 1980
Copyright © 1980 by Richard Ornberg

In Chicago, posters showing a picture of Mayor Jane Byrne with a target printed across her face are outselling similar posters depicting the Ayatollah Khomeini. Chants of "Burn, Witch Byrne" set the cadence for the first firefighter strike picket-line in the history of the city.

The third major strike to hit Chicago within a year had engaged the city administration in battle with the Chicago Firefighters Union, Local No.2, the second largest firefighters' union in the country.

Union President Frank "Moon" Muscare won his second attempt to secure a strike authorization vote in December 1979 after the union voted down a similar attempt one year before. The second vote followed a strike by transportation employees and a teachers strike, both of which last several days.

The firefighters' strike, however, resulted in heated and controversial debates between the union and the city, debates within the press, and, most of all, agonizing debates between firefighters over the difficult decision: "walk," or "stay in."

The question facing each firefighter was one of loyalties and goals. One was to the city for which they worked, and the other was to the union that struggled to obtain a contract and protections that had never before been specified in writing. For 23 days, firefighters, engineers, paramedics, and officers fought. shed tears, lost sleep, and wondered: what is happening?

The firefighter's union had endorsed the candidacy of Jane Byrne after she had promised, during her campaign, that the firefighters would receive a written contract. Jane Byrne was elected, beating the strong "machine" that had offered Michael Bilandic for a second term. Bilandic's defeat was blamed mainly on the ineptness of the city to provide adequate snow removal during the blizzard of 1979 and, then, at least as voters perceived it, lying about the city's inability to remove the snow.

The main issues in a contract desired by the union would have directly affected most of the city's 4,350 firefighters. The majority are members of the union, about 95 percent of the force, and includes officers. They man 120 firehouses throughout the city, housing 107 engines, 60 ladder trucks, 107 flying squads, nearly 40 ambulances, and 3 fireboats.

The union wanted all members to be covered under the contract, including all officers up to, but not including, the fire commissioner and his three deputies. The union also wanted an increase in manpower on responding apparatus, from four men on an engine to five, and six men on all ladder trucks. They wanted an immediate increase, with the initial boosts to be accomplished by hiring new men and paying them overtime. The union said they would agree to a "no strike" clause only for the life of the contract. They wanted final and binding arbitration with one arbitrator.

Salary increases, though small and unconventional, were demanded, but it was assumed that the most important items were: (1) existence of a contract (without interference by city ordinances), (2) the inclusion of officers in the bargaining unit, and (3) manpower increases. The city offered to man half the rigs with additional manpower by March 31, 1980, by hiring 250 new firefighters. They demanded a perpetual "no strike" clause, and wanted three arbitrators for binding arbitration.

Resisting the demand to include officers in the bargaining unit, the city felt supervisory personnel should not be considered as anything but management personnel. They feared the union would control the department.

As the strike evolved, so did the issues. Each side alternately withdrew and reinstated demands for binding arbitration under various conditions. The question of "amnesty" became the primary point as the strike neared several unfulfilled settlements. It was the repeated "flip-flopping" on the issues and the matter of amnesty that broke down negotiations, or chances for substantive talks.

With all civil service protections withdrawn by Mayor Daley a few years before, many firefighters felt that politics was playing too large a role in both entrance and promotions, as well as in disciplinary actions. They felt a contract would solve these problems and had believed Jane Byrne when she had promised a contract.

Said one firefighter: "She's trying to back out of her

commitment to give us collective bargaining. The original contract she handed us was unbelievable. We'll negotiate everything, for instance, and then everything is subject to the collective bargaining ordinance. If we agree on six men on the apparatus and the ordinance comes out and says five men, we'll have five men."

The union threatened to strike unless the city agreed to sit down and negotiate a contract free of outside interference. "No more handshakes, baby," insisted Muscare. "We want it on paper."

In a handout preparing union members for a strike, the union claimed the ordinance was a "union-busting tactic." Noting that the city had retained the firm of Seyfarth, Shaw, Fairweather, and Geraldson (accomplished, pro-management labor lawyers), the handout stated: "These ordinances are designed to create the illusion of collective bargaining, while stacking the deck against real and meaningful negotiations."

A strike groundwork had been laid. Headquarters were opened, strike chairmen assigned, and meetings were held with suburban union officials to try and deter efforts by the city to break an eventual strike with suburban firefighting forces (see sidebar, "Unmutual Aid").

This action prompted the city to begin talks with the union, and negotiations were underway. The specter of the collective bargaining ordinance broke these talks down early in the effort and a strike was threatened again.

This time pickets were printed. The battle through the press began with the city maintaining it had a "contingency plan" that included strike-breakers, the Illinois National Guard, and suburban support to deal with basic fire protection of the city. The union was steadfast in their claims that a strike would pull over 90 percent of the work force out on the street, including officers.

Fire Commissioner Richard Albrecht called the union "irresponsible" and remarked: "As far as I'm concerned, we're ready for any problem that could occur. We're ready to keep citizens protected."

The city rejected an offer by the union of what was called a "realistic strike plan" that would provide authorized union strikers to man rigs and still maintain protection for the city for the duration of the strike. The union wanted control of the department until an agreement was reached and ratified by both sides in the dispute.

Talks resumed and broke down. Again Muscare met with his membership and executive board. The decision was finally made to strike. The order came down to walk at 5:15 A.M. on February 14, Valentine's Day. Firefighters left the stations with their helmets, boots, and bunker coats and formed the first picket lines ever to march in front of Chicago firehouses. The union claimed fl 87 -percent walkout and the city countered with figures closer to 50 percent. Some stations were virtually abandoned as total walkouts occurred throughout the city. Many stations housed no more than a few officers and recruits fresh out of the academy.

The mayor and fire commissioner went on television to assure the residents of Chicago that all the houses were manned and that there was no need for panic. The police department cancelled all days off for officers. Extra patrols were put on the street and cars were assigned to each firehouse.

In an emotional plea, Commission Albrecht called for firefighters to return to work. "The men of the fire department took an oath of office to protect the lives of citizens," he said. "I expect them to obey the court order and return to work."

When Mayor Byrne learned of the walkout, she secured a court order from Circuit Judge John Hechinger. Calling it a "very, very sad day for the City of Chicago, and a sad day for the fire department," she added that "anyone who doesn't return to work will never again work for the Chicago Fire Department. Never. If they walk off this job, they can forget they were ever members of the fire department."

Holding a document informing firefighters they were violating a court order, Frank Muscare told a rally outside City Hall, "This is a Valentine from Jane Byrne. Can we send her one back?" The crowd of hundreds of firefighters cheered their approval of the disdainful Muscare. "I will go to jail if necessary!" shouted Muscare. Though he didn't know it at the time, the statement was prophetic.

The battle over how many walked out and how many stayed in began immediately. Both sides looked for statistical support. The city pointed to 1100 lunches that were ordered out during the first day as an indication of manpower. (Non-strikers were not allowed to leave the stations to go shopping, and, according to Capt. Jim Simpson of Flying Squad No.7, while there was no initial vandalism apparent, "some of the stoves were dismantled just before the walkout.")

"Show me a fireman who only eats one sandwich," argued one striking firefighter. "Besides, they're feeding all the city worker scabs they called in for support." Street and sanitation workers were ordered to respond with apparatus to fire scenes and offer support services for non-striking firefighters.

The National Guard was not called in. Illinois Governor James Thompson agreed that the strike was illegal, but added: "The Illinois National Guard is not trained to fight fires, and will not fight fires. They will not enter burning buildings."

Mayor Byrne called the strikers "lawbreakers" and said that she would not negotiate while firefighters were on the street. Fire Commissioner Albrecht set up a command center at the fire academy and directed operations as fire apparatus was put back in service and rearranged throughout the city.

O'Hare International Airport, a major priority to both the union and the city, was allowed to remain open after Federal Aviation Administration officials inspected the stations and equipment that were manned by supervisory personnel.

What would it take to return the firefighters to duty? Said strike chairman William Kugelman: "First to re-open negotiations. Then to secure a signed contract."

In an attempt to move things along, Mayor Byrne visited several of the fire stations and spoke face to face with picketers. At one point during a "sidewalk debate," she told one striking paramedic that the city had agreed to include lieutenants in the bargaining and might even include captains. The paramedic responded that if she would "put it in writing" he would return to duty. After a few seconds, she waved her arm and said, "C'mon up." This short blurb was enough to get both parties back to the table. At least for awhile.

A "no strike" clause was discussed, with the union agreeing to a "no strike" provision during the life of the contract. The city demanded a "no strike" agreement up front. Without the ability to strike at the end of the contract, the union felt they would have little or no bargaining power. The city said that Muscare kept changing the rules and the union said the city was lying.

Fires did break out and by the fourth day, several fires had been extinguished by both non-striking firefighters and strikers who left the picket lines and responded in their own cars, immediately returning to the picket lines after the fire was under control. Some strikers jeered and taunted firefighters who were fighting fires throughout the city. New recruits called up by Mayor Byrne were met at the fire academy by firefighters with pickets yelling, "You're gonna have to deal with us someday!" and "What do you want to go in there for? She's gonna fire you when it's over!"

The few firefighters and officers who stayed on duty remained at the firehouses for days, resting when they could. Non-striking paramedics slept on cots at local hospitals under police protection while strikers outside the fire stations chanted, "C'mon out. C'mon out." The city reported that some firefighters were returning to work, but others succumbed to the chants and left, joining the strikers. Those that left did so with tears in their eyes. They had tried to measure their own values and for various reasons altered them as the strike continued.

One non-striking firefighter had his reasons for staying in. "The fire department is my family," he explained. "My uncle died on the job, my father is a retired fireman. I've got two brothers in the department and one of them is striking. I don't know why."

It was clear that the strike was going to last longer than everyone had feared. The city requested a contempt of court citation against the union. Judge Hechinger called both the city and the union negotiators to the courtroom and tried to bring the two sides together. After failing in his own brand of "shuttle diplomacy," Hechinger issued the contempt citations and levied heavy fines on the union, Muscare, and other union officials who refused to order their men back to work. The fines totaled $40,000 a day. "We're not going to pay," said Muscare. "We might as well go to jail now."

Mayor Byrne vowed never to speak to Muscare or other union officials again, and ordered the immediate hiring and "crash training" of 2,500 new firefighters. The thought of firefighters assuming firefighting duties after a two week course infuriated the union and strikers.

When union officials were threatened with arrest, the Chicago Federation of Police threatened to call a strike.

International Association of Fire Fighters (IAFF)

Executive President Howie McClennan, a board member of the AFL-CIO, secured the support of the Chicago Federation of Labor through CFL President William Lee. The national AFL-CIO Executive Committee also voted support of the firefighters.

During another attempt at forcing talks, Judge Hechinger ordered both sides to report to his courtroom. Mayor Byrne reluctantly sent her negotiators. Also attending were CFL President Lee, teamster's chief Louis Peick and other labor leaders. Later that evening, the same labor leaders met with Mayor Byrne.

With the firefighters and the city in separate rooms, quickly dubbed "The Firehouse" and "The City," Judge Hechinger finally secured an agreement by which the firefighters would return to work the next morning, and the city would enter "around the clock" negotiations to settle the disputes. As a condition, total amnesty was promised striking firefighters.

For a short time spirits were high again, but caution was still the rule. The next morning, however, confusion began. Firefighters charged they were "locked out" and the city said that the union had not removed the pickets. "Hell," said one returning firefighter, "I came here at 7:30 this morning to go back to work. I came here because the union told me to go to work and not to picket, and then it got all screwed up."

One battalion chief raced to city hall in an engine, complete with flashing lights and siren yelping to complain to the mayor about the amnesty agreement. The strike was still on.

Judge Hechinger had had enough. He sentenced Muscare to five months in jail for contempt of court, citing his "big mouth." "The emotions of your men were strong to return to work," scolded Hechinger in a blast against the union president. "They had hope, Frank Muscare, which you doused. I'm not sure you ever wanted a contract...unless you got...your own terms."

More meetings were held between the city and the union (now represented by Acting President William Reddy and other officials). Muscare was kept abreast of the situation and even addressed a membership meeting over the phone from jail.

On February 22, a "Memorandum of Agreement" was reached between the city and union officials. Amnesty was included, and the other items in dispute were to be reviewed by a team of "fact finders." The meeting was arranged by CFL leaders and did not include union attorney J. Dale Berry, or International Association of Fire Fighters representative Michael Lass. The agreement was signed by Reddy for four other union officials.

When the agreement was presented to the full executive board, they had questions concerning certain provisions and refused to approve the memo until Mayor Byrne would clarify those points. Strike chairman Bill Kugelman said the city tried to push an agreement without proper representation for the union. Assured Kugelman: "They stuck our guys in there with the big guns and railroaded and ramrodded the agreement down their throats."

The agreement was finally rejected by the union after several labor leaders became involved and Bill Lee of the CFL refused to meet with the firefighters' union.

IAFF Executive President McClennan flew to Florida to meet AFL-CIO head Lance Kirkland to have pressure exerted on Lee to increase his support of the firefighters. Said McClennan: "All the firefighters feel he's been working closely with the mayor."

On February 26, the Federal Mediation and Conciliatory Service in Washington, D.C., sent mediator Edward

McMahon to Chicago. Mayor Byrne refused McMahon's request to get both sides to a meeting.

Over the next few days, little progress was made towards reaching any kind of a settlement. After several fire deaths, (which the city maintained were not caused by the strike) and the injuries of six firefighters at an extra-alarm blaze, the city began disciplinary action against many of the firefighters, calling for either suspensions or dismissals. Saying that the city "can do with fewer firefighters," the mayor called for a total reorganization of the fire department.

March 3 brought renewed and additional support from several local labor organizations, including the City Worker's Union, Cook County Teachers, the Steelworkers, and others. Political accusations continued to fly in the Mayor's direction from city aldermen charging Byrne with unreasonable tactics and refusing to talk to the union. Mayor Byrne agreed to meet with IAFF Secretary/ Treasurer Frank Palumbo. CFL head Lee said that while he felt the union leadership was not accurately informing their membership, he hoped that the meeting between Palumbo and Mayor Byrne could re-open negotiations.

The mayor agreed to new talks but this time refused to grant total amnesty for strikers. A membership meeting was held, and 3,500 firefighters rejected the latest proposal. Attending the meeting was Reverend Jesse Jackson, the civil rights leader who himself had led many equal rights demonstrations over the years. At the meeting, Jackson pledged his efforts towards reaching an agreement, stating that his concern was primarily for those minorities who suffered the greatest losses from fire.

Mayor Byrne surprisingly allowed Jackson to serve as mediator in what her husband/press secretary Jay McMullen termed "a last ditch effort to settle the strike."

After a 12-hour session with Jackson serving as mediator, a tentative agreement was reached and a special midnight membership meeting was scheduled. The membership unanimously accepted the agreement.

Firefighters returned to work the next morning with an agreement of limited amnesty that required all striking firefighters to forfeit from one to four days without pay, depending upon their rank. The strikers would also lose pay for the time they were on strike.

In return the firefighters were guaranteed all rights and privileges they had had prior to the strike, and that all items in dispute would be submitted to a five-man fact-finding team. If the team's recommendations were not acceptable, negotiations would resume for another two months. Then, remaining items would be submitted to binding arbitration, with the city able to reject the settlement. If rejected, the union could call another strike after giving 10 days notice.

The city agreed to beef up the manpower on apparatus during the interim periods (five firefighters on all trucks and one-half of the engines in 1980, and the balance in 1981) and agreed to a new grievance procedure. The issue of officers being included in the bargaining was submitted to fact-finding.

During the strike, 22 people died, including fire victims and emergency medical cases. Each time a fire death was reported – whether four children unable to escape, or medical emergencies that arrived DOA – questions arose concerning response time and efficiency of personnel.

After each emergency that resulted in a tragedy, the city insisted that the deaths were "unavoidable," and made efforts to point out the short response times in each instance. Bystanders, on the other hand, claimed time lapses of 15 to 20 minutes between the time of the fire and the arrival of fire or medical equipment.

According to the Cook County Medical Examiner's office, during the same time period in the year 1979, 26 deaths caused by fire were recorded. In the same time period in 1978, the figure was 13.

Some of the firefighters were questioning just how Reverend Jackson's help finally produced an agreement. Strike chairman Bill Kugelman said it wasn't all Jackson. "Sure, he represents a lot of minorities in Chicago, but there were at least 50 other religious organizations that were about to lower the boom on Jane Byrne. There was a lot of pressure being applied. She was getting calls from Kennedy [Senator Edward M. Kennedy had just visited the city as part of his presidential primary campaign] and some others."

Returning firefighters, while all happy about going back to work, offered different feelings. "We're firemen again!" shouted one smiling firefighter. "Great to be back," remarked another. A non-striker, Deputy Chief Edwin Nelson was apprehensive. Said he: "Everyone's a loser in this one. We do our housework together. We fight fires together. We socialize together. This has ripped the family apart. How are we to overcome this feeling?" Noted another firefighter: "There might be some silent treatment for awhile, but time heals."

The strike cost the city an estimated $16-million. Although the city saved salaries that were not paid striking firefighters, it had to pay the overtime earned by firefighters who remained, police, sanitation, and street workers who substituted, and the cost of feeding those who continued on the job. Extra fuel was used by police squads and new firefighting turnouts had to be purchased to supply newly hired recruits that the city had not budgeted for.

Outside the last membership meeting that resulted in the final ratification of an agreement, two firefighters were patting each other on the back after a 23-day emotional nightmare. Said one: "We showed her that we can do it." Replied the other, still smiling, "Yeah, but it'll take an atomic bomb to get me out of that station next time."

Training for Shuttle Blastoff

Published, *FIREHOUSE Magazine*, March, 1986

It was less than two hours before the launch of the Space Shuttle Challenger. The huge spacecraft hung like a large ornament on the even larger booster rockets that would carry a crew of eight astronauts - the most ever to be placed into orbit at one time-into a 200-mile-high orbit around the Earth.

The "Close Out" crew had already left the pad and retreated with all other personnel to safe locations more than three miles away. The astronauts, in position aboard the orbiter, sat alone atop thousands of pounds of cryogenics, hypergolic fuels and solid booster propellants, some of which were still being pumped into fuel tanks.

Though everyone had been evacuated from the launch

pad area at Florida's Kennedy Space Center (KSC), seven firefighters stood by along with an M113 Armored Personnel Carrier at a point known as A-5, less than a mile away. Dressed in thermal underwear, Nomex and other protective layers, with compressed air supply bottles held in hand and strapped to their legs, the "A-5 Pad Rescue Team" baked in the midday sun of October 25, 1985.

Nearby, at the Shuttle Landing Facility, additional teams of fire personnel, groups of volunteers making up several Off Site Contingency Operations (OSCO) Teams, stood by with their equipment, ready to be airlifted by helicopter to the site of an emergency landing of an aborted mission vehicle. Fire crash trucks and ambulances stood by at various locations, as the countdown to launch continued. Two additional M-113s, fully manned, also stood by to aid in any rescue attempt required at Launch Pad 39A.

This ready posture was started at least six hours before the scheduled noon launch, until four minutes and 23 seconds after Challenger cleared the pad. If, after that time, a problem develops with one of the thousands of systems and the mission is aborted, there can be no return to the Kennedy Space Center for a landing. The orbiter must proceed to another contingency site-Dakar, Senegal in West Africa, for example-where another KSC rescue team, dispatched days earlier from the space center, will be standing by.

On this particular launch, the liftoff came without a hitch or delay, just another routine activity for the members of the Kennedy Space Center Fire and Rescue Service. They had to extinguish only a few small brush fires, remainders of the fiery ignition that had occurred.

Surprisingly, the word "routine" applies to most KSC activities. Shuttle launches, averaging almost one per month, and the related activities throughout the space center have become routine, but the 100 plus members of the fire and rescue service have not become complacent.

The Kennedy Space Center is a sprawling futuristic complex located on the central Atlantic coast of Florida. Covering 140,000 acres and containing a population that varies from 14,000 to 16,000 employees, the complex is like a city in itself. On any launch day, when the population can swell to 40,000 observers and members of the press, 7,000 or more automobiles and 300 busloads of VIPs, the KSC Fire Department's responsibility rivals that of a department in a large U.S. city.

KSC Fire Chief Richard Cross is quick to point out that the majority of the KSC activities can be considered support and standby. Many different types of hazards exist at the center, which include supplies, movements and storage of helium and nitrogen (used for inert purging of lines, pressurization and leak checking during pre-launch operations and onboard propellant tank pressurants); cryogens like liquid oxygen and liquid hydrogen (used as the primary launch propellants by the orbiter); and the primary hypergolic propellants, fuels and oxidizers that ignite on contact with each other - like monomethylhydrazine and nitrogen tetroxide (used in the orbiter's secondary propulsion systems for orbital maneuvering).

During the various test firings of engines (called "Hotfires"), fueling operations, the incoming and outgoing of special aircraft at the Shuttle Landing Facility and other sensitive activities, KSC fire personnel are called upon to stand by and support procedures with appropriate firefighting and rescue equipment. The scheduling of these standby and support services account for the bulk of KSC fire activities.

The KSC Fire Department is also charged with the protection of all structures within the space center, but, according to Chief Cross, - a 25-year veteran of the Washington, D.C. Fire Department serving his last six years as a battalion chief - the built-in fire suppression systems are extensive. "There are a tremendous amount of built-in detection and suppression systems out here," says the chief. "More than any place I've ever seen. If every city had it, you probably wouldn't need fire departments. There are sprinkler systems, Halon systems, fixed dry powder systems, heat, smoke and gas detectors, low oxygen sensors just everywhere."

Such extensive protection systems, however, prove to be more cost effective at the space center than in many other locations. "We've done an extensive risk analysis for every major facility out here," explains Cross. "One was just done on the Orbiter Processing Facility, basically a hanger-like facility where they work on the orbiters. That one risk analysis report had a dollar-loss figure of $1 billion. That was for the building and one orbiter. Now that's just for one building."

"What concerns me more from a structural standpoint are buildings like the NASA Headquarters building next door to us here," adds the chief. "I came from Washington, D.C., where I've fought some horrendous fires in offices. Now people think that's no big deal, but they've been some of the worst fires I've pulled up on. In fact, they had one in D.C. last winter that was a hundred million dollars."

Chief Cross also expresses understandable concern in more typical fire protection areas like several trailer complexes on the center and several temporary offices located throughout the complex. He has assigned officers to preplan the buildings from a firefighting standpoint and to develop attack plans.

The KSC Fire and Rescue Service is a division of EG & G Florida, a private contractor. To handle most of the center's base operations, the EG & G work force and subcontractors now number approximately 2000. Formerly fulfilled by

13 separate contractors, the department's responsibilities include activities like designing sophisticated systems for delivering rocket fuels to space vehicles, taking care of roads, grounds, buildings, base security, and, of course, providing fire protection.

The KSC Fire Department consists of 13 officers, 64 firefighters, 20 firefighter/ paramedics and an inspection team of eight fire inspectors, three inspection technicians and a fire marshal. The fire inspectors ensure that all codes are either met or exceeded throughout the complex, especially in connection with so many exotic, explosive and toxic materials.

In addition to three Armored Personnel Carriers, the department's apparatus consists of three 1250-gpm pumpers, each carrying 500 gallons of water; a 1000-gpm pumper; a 95-foot aerial tower, also with a 1000-gpm pump; two older pumpers used as spares and backups, four crash/fire/rescue trucks and two 250-gpm minipumpers.

Certified paramedics along with six mobile intensive care units provide emergency medical services for the base, its employees and visitors, and also provide a sense of security for on-site technicians, engineers and astronauts. Their telemetry communications, a direct by-product of the space program itself, is handled through the KSC Occupational Health Facility. But the Fire and Rescue Service really kicks into high gear before each launch of a space shuttle. Days before the launch, work schedules are altered, off duty personnel are scheduled for launch day activities and preparations, and every contingency operation is reviewed through "walk-throughs," chalkboard simulations and on-site reviews.

Under the direction of 20-year KSC veteran and Training Officer Captain George Hoggard, who acts as the Pad Rescue Team Leader, six firefighters stand by each mile from the base of Launch Pad 39A. Chief Cross describes the scenario. "About six hours prior to the launch of a space shuttle, we deploy a rescue team at the position called the 'A-5 roadblock.' That's about one mile from the launch pad itself. We go out there six hours before because there are a lot of people out there working. There is a close-out crew on site, and the ice inspection team. As the cryogenics are loaded, they're super cold, and the condensation and humidity here in Florida cause ice buildup. The crew performs a visual inspection to assure that the buildup is not excessive. We're out there in case there is a propellant leak. Should they be exposed to a toxic substance or become incapacitated, we can effect a rescue."

Cross says that when the ice inspection team leaves, firefighters and apparatus at the pad gate "fall back" and leave the close-out crew to await the astronauts' arrival. Once the astronauts have been positioned inside the orbiter, the close-out crew closes the hatch, seals the orbiter and leaves the structure. The A-5 team becomes the closest help available during the last one-and-a-half to two hours of the countdown.

"If something happens out there [on the launch pad] that incapacitates the flight crew or remaining close-out crew so they cannot function on their own to escape the structure, then we are called to go in," explains Cross. "The rescue crew responds to the pad in the M-113 (Armored Personnel Carrier), which can go about 40 mph. The members get on the elevator and ride to the 195-foot level, where they can access the orbiter hatch where the crew enters. Drawing from a rescue locker nearby, they pull out a hatch tool and rescue chair and proceed through the 'White Room.' Two members of the rescue crew then enter the orbiter and go directly to the flight deck." Using a metal sliding board that fits from the hatch opening down to the edge of the pilot's seat, the rescuers unhook the straps that restrain the astronauts and physically slide the pilot and other crew members up and out of the orbiter. They place the astronauts into a rescue chair, take them to the opposite side of the structure and put them into a large rescue "basket" that holds up to five people. A device called a "Guillotine Cutter" is used to cut the restraining rope holding the basket in place. The basket slides down a metal wire cable to ground level at a distance of a quarter-mile away from the pad. There are five such baskets available for use, and each is caught just above ground level by large webbing or nets. The victims can then be transferred to a nearby "Slidewire Bunker" or be placed into other M-113s that respond to the base of the slidewire.

Each astronaut receives training by KSC fire personnel in the operation of the M-113s, in case they must use the escape method on their own. In any case, the last basket is reserved for rescue personnel. "Actually, we're only involved if the astronauts are unable to help themselves. They know the procedures, and if they have to move out, they will," says the chief.

If all goes well and the launch is successful, fire teams then respond to the pad area to extinguish any small brush or grass fires that may have resulted. These are minor, says Cross, but since they can occur near some of the fueling lines and tanks, they need to be taken care of.

"Then the pad has to be 'safed,' " continues the chief. Environmental Health teams will eventually go directly to the pad and check for broken fuel or gas lines using mechanical "sniffers." Adds Cross: "We back up these crews, who also walk the structure, checking for damage.

"Should there be a problem after the launch, however-for example, if they weren't getting full power from the engines, and a 'Return To Launch Site' (RTLS) is declared, then the

OSCO Team goes into action."

OSCO is made up of teams of KSC Fire and Rescue Service volunteers, including two women. Their skills come into play in the event of a declared RTLS within four minutes and 23 seconds. (After that time, speed and distance dictate that another predetermined contingency landing site must be used.) If the orbiter must return to KSC, rescue teams have 22 minutes to wait. It takes that long for the shuttle to jettison its boosters and make a wide circle in order to reduce air speed from nearly 16,000 mph to approximately 220 mph for a landing attempt at the Shuttle Landing Facility. "If all goes well, the shuttle should be able to effect a landing at the airstrip," explains Cross. "Should the shuttle overshoot or undershoot the landing strip, it can come down anywhere in the Atlantic, in the waterways or along the coast of Florida."

The chief explains that the craft may come down either right or left of the runway as well. "Since last winter, there haven't been any scheduled landings at the KSC landing facility," says Cross. "Since the pilot must steer the craft with his brakes, we've had a couple of tires blow on landing. Recently a steering capability was developed, and in all probability the landings will resume here at KSC about the beginning of the year."

During those 22 minutes, a helicopter will act as a spotter. Once it determines a location for the downed craft, additional choppers airlift the OSCO teams along with their equipment to the site. If the craft lands in water, the teams are dropped into the water a safe distance from the orbiter to avoid any possible ignition of escaping vapors. The OSCO teams paddle to the orbiter and, with teams on both sides of the cockpit area, throw a messenger line over the top of the craft. Using this line, rescuers hoist a Jacobs Ladder so they can reach the hatch and gain entry. During this time the teams communicate with each other with CO_2 airhorns, as radios are difficult to use in water. The rescuers remove the crew members, place them in Stokes baskets and then paddle away so they can be retrieved by the helicopters.

If the craft ends up on land, the teams are transported by chopper to the site and left nearby. Each chopper carries the complete rescue pack and equipment for each team. The first pack consists of two Stokes baskets, a life raft and oars, a Jacobs Ladder and messenger line, hatch tools, high-intensity chemical lights, additional air bottles, CO_2 air horns and radio vectors that send out a continuing signal for other teams to home in on.

Though NASA officials contend that the orbiter should float in water, OSCO teams train with the belief that the orbiter may sink very rapidly or, at the very least, nose up, depending on the payload, the depth of the water and other factors. In either case, training is based on the worst case scenario.

Under the direction of OSCO Rescue Chief Barry Davidson, the teams practice, check out and pack the various rescue packs they will take with them to the site. Under the shadow of the Mate/DeMate Device, used to place or remove the orbiter from the Boeing 747 used for shuttle transport, the OSCO teams inspect and pack all equipment.

In addition to carrying rescue packs, the choppers can also transport ladders, hose-lines, floating portable 250-gpm pumps and other equipment in a separate pack that can be slung underneath the helicopter. The portable water tank can be filled by the choppers using tanks ferried from a water site to the orbiter site in forest firefighting fashion, suspended under the helicopter.

Prior to each launch, the OSCO teams and other KSC firefighters brush up on procedures to be followed using a mockup shuttle cockpit located near the press site complex.

The mock-up can either be laid on its belly, to simulate a ground landing, or tipped vertically, to resemble its posture on the launch pad itself. Or the entire structure can be placed in an adjacent waterway, so crews can practice water rescues with all the necessary equipment.

For almost every launch so far, Chief Cross adds, an additional OSCO team is dispatched to the contingency landing" site in Dakar, Senegal, in West Africa. "It's right on the beach, and the guys say it's pretty nice. They like to go there." says the chief. "But this time it's not there. Since Spacelab flights are placed into a different orbit than usual, the contingency site is in Spain. There, a U.S. Air Force Base handles any emergency landings." Beginning in September of this year, when some of the launches will originate from Vandenberg Air Force Base, the alternate landing sites will be on either Easter Island or Hau, near Tahiti in the South Pacific.

Training isn't restricted to rescue operations, however. Elsewhere on the base is a special fire training site that includes a mock-up aircraft fuselage, for aircraft fire fighting training, and a fuel-burning pit, for crews to practice containment and extinguishment of fuel fires. One pit, specially constructed for the out-of-the ordinary fuels used at KSC, is situated in the midst of protective bunkers. Hypergolic fuels are introduced into the pit from opposite sides. As they meet they ignite, resulting in a series of rapid explosions that allow the orbiter to maneuver while in space.

The members of the Kennedy Space Center Fire and Rescue Service are proud of the part they play in the space program. The hours are long and training must sometimes be done before or after shifts, due to the heavy and continuous schedule. According to the chief, overtime must be used to provide adequate protection and service at times. A single launch, for example, can cost $1500 in overtime alone, since the shift complement must at times be doubled. Once, when various conditions required a hold of three continuous days, and ready postures had to be maintained, the overtime cost came to nearly $25,000.

Whether the responsibilities of fire and rescue services are as routine as inspections and standby or as critical as the rescue of astronauts, the men and women of the Kennedy Space Center Fire and Rescue Service are well aware of the special part they play both in the fire service and in mankind's ever-increasing expansion into the last real frontier.

About the author

Rick Ornberg served as fulltime firefighter with Des Plaines Fire Department from 1971-1996 as Firefighter, Acting Company Officer and on the Fire Prevention Bureau coordinating Fire and Burn Prevention Education. Contributed toward creation and launch of city's first Paramedic program in early 1970's, and was a frequent contributor to Firehouse Magazine and other associated trade publications.

A published freelance writer since 1979, Rick founded Ornberg & Associates in 1985, while still a fulltime firefighter. On his days off, Rick honed his skills and gained experience as a freelance writer while providing part time layout, design, writing and photography services as a "one-stop" provider for a wide variety of clients including businesses, organizations and political campaigns.

Retiring from the Fire Department in 1996 after 26 years of service, Ornberg & Associates expanded its client list providing collateral materials, print ads, newsletter and directory publishing services. Major clients included school districts, township government, national and international business associations, small and large corporations and local, state and national political campaigns.

In May, 2000, Rick took the helm as Executive Director of a large, 600-member Chamber of Commerce as an advocate for businesses, monitoring legislation, helping members with both marketing and networking, and learning about a wide variety of business disciplines and challenges.

In January, 2006, Rick rekindled his business as Eagle Mountain Promotions, providing quality promotional products, advertising specialties, imprinted apparel, fire prevention and business printing .

www.EagleMountainPromotions.com

Made in the USA
Lexington, KY
21 September 2012